# Culture Change

ELEMENTS OF ANTHROPOLOGY
*A Series of Introductions*

# Culture Change

*Clyde M. Woods*

University of California
Los Angeles

WM. C. BROWN COMPANY PUBLISHERS
Dubuque, Iowa

**ANTHROPOLOGY SERIES**

Consulting Editors

*Frank Johnston*
*University of Pennsylvania*

*Henry Selby*
*Temple University*

*For Jeffrey and Michael*

# Contents

# Preface

Although the study of change has occupied an important place in anthropological thought and activity over the years, it has not yet received the attention it warrants. This is reflected in the literature available on the subject: articles, chapters, and case studies abound, while comprehensive treatments of change as a subdiscipline are practically nonexistent and good, predictive theory is seriously lacking. This deficiency is particularly unfortunate at this point in history when the pace of change accelerates dramatically with each new decade. Anthropologists and other social scientists can no longer take a passive role in simply studying the *consequences* of change. There is growing acceptance of the notion that we must apply our special knowledge and skills in an attempt to ease the commonly disruptive effects of such worldwide events as development, modernization, industrialization, and urbanization. To be successful in this endeavor we must first further our own understanding of the actual *processes* of change through more systematic, multi-disciplinary, and theoretically relevant investigations in a variety of different settings. Only then will useful, predictive theories evolve which can be used to guide programs of change that ease the transition to new technologies, lifestyles, and states of mind.

This monograph can do little to fill the void in the literature nor is that its intent. It is meant, rather, to stimulate an awareness and interest in the subject by introducing the reader to basic principles, ideas, approaches, and examples of the subdiscipline. Hopefully, armed with these basics, the student of change will be encouraged to pursue a more thorough understanding of the topic through both the advanced literature and personal experience.

My own interest in the study of change was stimulated when Benjamin and Lois Paul brought me and my family to the midwestern highlands of Guatemala so that I might study the introduction of modern medicine into the Mayan Indian community of San Lucas Tolimán on Lake Atitlán. After a year in the lake region, I was firmly convinced that it was an ideal natural laboratory for the study of individual and community change over time and thus returned in 1969 to initiate such a study in fourteen towns. Materials from both the San Lucas and regional studies are included in this monograph. I am deeply indebted to Ben and Lois Paul for introducing me to the region and providing intellectual guidance. Father Gregory Schaffer in San Lucas Tolimán and Father Ramón Carlin in Santiago Atitlán offered countless acts of kindness and aid to me and my family during initial and succeeding field periods and Manuel Crespo Garcia of Panajachel has provided invaluable aid and friendship over the years. Flavio Rojas Lima of the Seminario de Integración Sociál Guatemalteca has kindly provided official sanction for the ongoing research project.

Native assistants and informants, along with research assistants from the Department of Anthropology, University of California, Los Angeles are too numerous to list in this context but have obviously been essential to such a long-range program. Several project personnel, however, deserve special mention in that they directly contributed to the present work. Laura Stein coded and punched much of the questionnaire data and William T. Farrell has provided indispensable aid in coordinating and processing project materials from 1969 to the present. Along with Farrell, Margo-Lea Hurwicz helped research materials and Clay H. Felts, Jr. processed some of the data in the final two chapters. Special thanks are in order for Margaret M. Kieffer who read and edited the manuscript and the series editor Henry A. Selby.

Clyde M. Woods
Panajachel, Guatemala

# Introduction

The study of change has been a major concern of anthropology since its inception as a scientific discipline about two centuries ago. This concern has increased considerably in recent years as anthropologists and other social scientists have focused more and more on the problems faced by Third World peoples as they make the often difficult transition to a more modern way of life. Culture change has been generally defined as " . . .any modification in the way of life of a people, whether consequent to internal developments or to contact between two peoples with unlike ways of life."[1] Changes attributed to internal developments are usually traced to discovery or invention while those attributed to external developments, or contact, are generally traced to borrowing or diffusion.

Most anthropologists today would agree that such changes are inevitable although there has been some attention devoted to cultural stability, or the tendency to remain the same. Early studies suggested that some societies were in a state of more or less perfect equilibrium or stability where the forces of change were subverted by those of cultural conservatism. While this may be more true for small, isolated, underdeveloped groups than for larger, industrialized, urbanized societies, it is now generally accepted that change is a constant in all cultures and social systems.

Culture remains the central concept in anthropology. An early definition proposed that culture was " . . .that complex whole which includes knowledge, belief, art, morals, custom and any other capabilities acquired by man as a member of society."[2] This definition is sufficiently broad to cover just about everything and herein lies its basic flaw—if culture is "everything" then it has no utility as either a descriptive or explanatory concept. More recent conceptualizations have been less general but vary greatly according to the orientation and intent of the definer.[3] A simple and concise definition is one that proposes culture as " . . .the integrated system of learned behavior patterns which are characteristic of the members of a society and which are not the result of biological inheritance."[4] In other words, culture is

1. Louise S. Spindler and George D. Spindler, "Culture Change," in *Biennial Review of Anthropology* B. J. Siegel, ed. (Stanford: Stanford University Press, 1959), p. 37.

2. Edward B. Tylor, *Primitive Culture* (Boston: Estes and Lauriat, 1874).

3. Alfred L. Kroeber and Clyde Kluckhohn identified 500 different uses of the culture concept in reviewing the literature. See their book, *Culture: A Critical Review of Concepts and Definitions*, Peabody Museum Papers 47,1 (Cambridge: Harvard University Press, 1952).

4. E. Adamson Hoebel, *Anthropology: The Study of Man*, 4th ed. (New York: McGraw-Hill, Inc., 1972), p. 6.

passed on from generation to generation through the process of socialization, is shared by members of the group, and its essential features vary from society to society.

So conceptualized, the concept has obvious descriptive merits but two shortcomings remain. First of all, the concept is still too broad to be useful as an explanatory construct. In other words, to say that the Americans and the French are different because they have different cultures does not explain *how* and *why* they are different. Culture in this broad sense cannot be measured. Second, and closely related, is the fact that by concentrating on behavior patterns which are *characteristic* of the group, the culture concept automatically implies a postulate of homogeneity. That is, if it is proposed that people are the way they are because of their culture then it follows that they are more or less exact replicas of their culture—and one another.[5] Used in this way, individual variability in behavior, attitudes, and beliefs can, and has been, largely ignored. You need only to look around you to see that you are not a mirror image of your cultural, or even subcultural, companions.

Ward Goodenough has led a pioneering effort in attempting to resolve these conceptual difficulties.[6] He suggests that anthropologists and others have blurred the important distinction between culture as patterns *of* behavior and culture as patterns *for* behavior and often use the two meanings interchangeably. In the former case culture refers to the "way of life" and in the latter to the "design" for that way of life. This is reflected in a commonly cited definition which concludes that "...culture systems may, on the one hand, be considered as *products* of action, and on the other as *conditioning elements* of further action."[7] [emphasis added] In view of these problems, Goodenough proposes that the culture concept can best be uti-

lized as a mental construct—a sort of cognitive map which provides the individual with appropriate rules for behavior in various situational contexts. Some of these "rules" are idiosyncratic to the individual, some are shared with some members of the group, and others are shared with most members of the group.[8] Those which are shared with most members of the society *lead to* "behavior patterns characteristic of the group" and comprise culture in the traditional sense. So culture is shared but not completely. Individual variability can be recognized.

From this point of view culture change consists of modifications in these rules *and* the behavioral correlates they prescribe. Both can be measured using standardized techniques available to the anthropologist. This conceptualization also focuses on the real unit of change—the individual. Anthropologists, of course, are not unaware that the individual is the basic mechanism of change. Many though, have tended to couch their explanations in relatively abstract cultural terms. This is true of much of the literature we will review in the proceeding pages, and as such,

5. For what is perhaps the most extreme example of the use of the "homogeneity postulate," see, Ruth Benedict, *Patterns of Culture* (Boston: Houghton Mifflin Company, 1934). And for a general critique which refers to this postulate as the "replication of uniformity" and poses it against a preferred approach called the "organization of diversity," see, A.F.C. Wallace, *Culture and Personality*, 2nd ed. (New York: Random House, 1970).

6. See, Ward H. Goodenough, "Comment on Cultural Evolution," *Daedalus* 90 (1961): 521-8 and idem, *Cooperation in Change: An Anthropological Approach to Community Change* (New York: The Russell Sage Foundation, 1963).

7. Alfred L. Kroeber and Clyde Kluckhohn, *Culture: A Critical Review of Concepts and Definitions*, Peabody Museum Papers 47,1 (Cambridge: Harvard University Press, 1952), p. 181.

8. Goodenough refers to these different kinds of culture as *private*, *operational*, and *public* respectively.

we will use culture in both senses. We should, however, keep the distinction in mind. As a concept, culture has been used to both *describe* and *prescribe* behavior. The latter has explanatory properties. The former does not.

Culture change and social change are part and parcel of the same process but can be distinguished conceptually when necessary. Where culture may be defined as prescriptions for living, society refers to the organized aggregate of people who follow these prescriptions, and social system to the patterns of social interaction which occur. Social change refers to a modification in the structure or function of the social system. Examples would be a change in the structure of race relations, the elimination of class differences, or a change in the structure and function of the family. But note that these changes are accompanied by cultural changes. In the last example concerning the family, an increasing acceptance of abortion, family planning, job equality between the sexes, and nonlegalized marriages (culture changes) might well lead to smaller, less permanent families which are adult rather than child-oriented (social changes).

Since cultural and social changes are so closely related the distinction is commonly ignored and in the pages which follow we will often simply refer to sociocultural change. This does not mean that the distinction is not useful in some cases. One can obviously effect the other and it has been convincingly demonstrated that a lag in the rate of change in either can produce disruptive effects.[9]

This book is organized in such a way as to afford an orderly and logical introduction to the basic principles, approaches, and literature of culture change. Chapter one is devoted to the development of anthropological interest in change and is meant to place proceeding materials in appropriate historical perspective. In chapter two the basic process of how and why change occurs is discussed and in three particular attention is devoted to the most common source of change—borrowing or diffusion. The divergent manifestations and implications of acculturation are covered in chapter four while the special problems and approaches common to directed or applied change are considered in chapter five.

The final two chapters are concerned with the all-important approaches and issues surrounding community development and modernization. The firs presents the basic dimensions of these kinds of changes along with a brief discussion of how anthropologists approach the study of change. The second then focuses on one particular region in order to demonstrate the dynamics of community development and modernization and to further clarify the general processes of change.

9. See, for example, Clifford Geertz, "Ritual and Social Change: A Javanese Example," *American Anthropologist* 59 (1957): 32-54 and Evon Z. Vogt, "On the Concepts of Structure and Process in Cultural Anthropology," *American Anthropologist* 62 (1960): 18-33.

# 1 | Anthropology and Change in Historical Perspective

In 1860 Charles Darwin, aided by Thomas Huxley and others, defended his thesis on the *Origin of the Species* before a meeting of the British Association for the Advancement of Science. Prior to this the scriptures had been the ultimate source of explanations regarding the nature of man and the universe. In Ireland, an archbishop had even worked out a biblical chronology: the world was created in 4004 B.C. and the flood took place about 2500 years later.[1] But if all men had been created equal and in God's image as stated in Genesis, how were the clerics to explain the disgusting state of the savages discovered in the explorations which began in the sixteenth century? A theory of "degeneration" was proposed: all men had been created equal and in God's image but some, like the two unfortunates in the Garden of Eden, had fallen from God's grace and subsequently degenerated to their savage state.

Darwin's ideas concerning biological evolution and man's considerable antiquity were supported by the work of Charles Lyell who established the notion of geological stratification, and by the discovery of Neanderthal bones in conjunction with those of ancient animals. Lyell showed that different layers of the earth were of different ages so that the world could not have been created at one point in time, while the discovery of Neander-

thal bones dating back to the Pleistocene Period suggested that man too was of considerable antiquity. Darwin's theory of natural selection and the survival of the fit was also heavily influenced by Malthus' ideas concerning the relationship between population pressure and food supply, Lamarck's notions about the inheritance of acquired characteristics (later proved wrong), and Mendel's discovery of the genetic mechanisms of species adaptation.

Not to be outdone, however, the clerics responded to these heretic ideas with such things as the "sinking hypothesis": the remains of Neanderthal had simply sunk to lower layers of the earth to reach the lower depths and besides that Neanderthal Man was no more than a "physiological idiot." In spite of this kind of thinking and considerable opposition even from within "scientific" circles, Darwin's ideas were eventually accepted. Man and earth were both of considerable antiquity and man had evolved from other species through the process of natural selection. Armed with this scientific advance, anthropologists and other social scientists on the continent and in the United States rushed forth to translate the principles of biologi-

1. H. R. Hays, *From Ape to Angel: An Informal History of Social Anthropology* (New York: Alfred A. Knopf, 1958).

cal evolution into those of cultural evolution.

## CLASSICAL EVOLUTION

One of the first schools to enter this endeavor was championed by an Englishman, Edward B. Tylor (1832-1917) and an American, Lewis H. Morgan (1818-1881).[2] These pioneering anthropologists and others attempted to provide explanations which would account for the development of all cultures everywhere on the basis of single schemes. An example can be taken from the work of Morgan who proposed that all societies everywhere pass through the same stages—from savagery to barbarism to civilization. And, they do so in unilineal fashion: every culture progresses through the same predetermined stages in all parts of the world. This was explained by the fact that men everywhere share the same mental processes—referred to by the evolutionists as the "psychic unity of mankind." The method of proof for Morgan was the existence of a few technologically related traits present at each stage of progression. Savagery and barbarism, respectively without and with pottery, each consisted of three stages. The lower stage of savagery is hypothetically represented as a "caveman without fire" with rudimentary social organization and no systematic language. The middle stage is typified by the Australian aborigines who possessed fire, stone tools, fishing, and seasonal migration patterns while the Polynesians of the upper stage were similar but had the bow and arrow. The Iroquois with pottery and stable existence represented the lower stage of barbarism, the Zuni with domesticated plants and animals were typical of the middle, and the Homeric Greeks with their iron tools moved into the upper level of barbarism. Civilization enters with phonetic writing and is represented by the beginnings of twentieth-century European lifeways. Extant primitive groups were explained as somehow having been arrested in their development and therefore had not properly progressed to the next stage.[3]

Morgan was forced to rely on a very incomplete data base and many of his assumptions, along with those of the other unilineal evolutionists, have been consequently shown to be incorrect. While culture does evolve and there is some truth to the assumption of the "psychic unity of mankind," all cultures do not pass through the same unilinear stages, independent invention is vastly overestimated, and contact between peoples with resulting borrowing (or diffusion) of cultural traits is largely ignored. There is also a misrepresentation of data as Morgan and others of the world on the basis of an a priori scheme. In short, sweeping generalizations are made on the basis of a scant and unreliable data base. It has been suggested that Morgan's fame lay more in historical accident than in solid achievement: Marx and Engels picked up his scheme and added communism as a final and more progressive stage.[4]

A number of other unilinear evolutionary schemes were proposed. The evolution of culture from primitive to civilized was supposedly accompanied by the progression from magic to religion to science; from promiscuity to group marriage to polygamy to monogamy; from polytheism to monotheism; from community property to private property; and so on.

---

2. For examples of their work, see, Edward B. Tylor, *Primitive Culture* (Boston: Estes and Lauriat, 1874) and Lewis H. Morgan, *Ancient Society* (New York: Henry Holt and Company, 1877).

3. Morgan, *Ancient Society.*

4. Robert H. Lowie, *The History of Ethnological Theory* (New York: Holt, Rinehart and Winston, 1937).

## SCHOOLS OF DIFFUSION

Where the evolutionists built their grand schemes of cultural development on independent invention based on the psychic unity of mankind, the diffusionists based theirs on grand scale borrowing. They rejected the predetermined unilineal stages and inevitable progress of the classical evolutionists and saw man as more of a copycat than an inventor. Of the three generally recognized schools of diffusion, the English "pan Egyptian" school was the most extreme. Spearheaded by G. Elliot Smith and W. J. Perry the school proposed that since man was basically uninventive, culture must have developed only once under extremely favorable circumstances and then spread from there to the rest of the world.[5] These circumstances, they felt, existed only in ancient Egypt—where Smith just happened to be stationed in the diplomatic service for a number of years. The following anecdote of Smith's description of the development of Egyptian civilization is provided by Robert Lowie:

In 4000 B.C. religion and social organization, marriage and burial ceremonies, houses and clothes, all arts and crafts except those used to make hunting equipment, were lacking everywhere outside of Egypt and vicinity. Human beings, we learn, lived essentially like the anthropoid apes. The ancient Egyptians were favored by the growth of wild barley in their country, which led to its deliberate cultivation, the inundations of the Nile prompting the natives to imitate its process by irrigation. Having to store food, the people invented pottery and granaries, the latter evolving into dwellings. 'The leisure enjoyed by men who stored up food in their settled homes' was devoted to inventing basketry, matting, and weaving; and, incidentally, cattle came to be domesticated. Religion rose out of the embalmer's art: the king-engineer who controlled fate by accurately predicting the movements of the Nile was mummified and henceforth treated as immortal. The practices performed to ensure the royal corpse against corruption gave rise to drama and ceremonialism, to dancing and music, also stimulating architecture and carpentry.[6]

With the rise of navigation the elements of this civilization were spread throughout the world but became more and more diluted as they reached the outposts of mankind. Hence, primitives were accounted for by decadence, or a watered down version of civilization. As proof of their theory the pan-Egyptian scholars relied primarily on the existence of three basic diagnostic features: stone tombs, stone idols, and mummification. Since these features were all present in ancient Egypt they must have diffused from there to other parts of the world.

While this school did emphasize the importance of borrowing, they flatly denied the inventiveness of man. In addition, the time-sequence is not in accord with the archaeological record, they ignored the difficulty of exporting such things as agriculture, and could not establish the existence of all three diagnostic features in any single culture except Egypt. They also confounded the important difference between form and function in their use of these diagnostic traits as evidence of diffusion. For example, just because mummified bodies (form) are found in other parts of the world does not provide sufficient evidence that the practice was borrowed from Egypt where important rulers were purposely prepared for life in the hereafter (function). In some dry climates bodies are

5. For examples of their work, see, G. Elliot Smith, *In The Beginning: The Origin of Civilization* (London: G. Howe Ltd., 1928) and W. J. Perry, *Children of The Sun* (London: Metheuw and Company, 1923).

6. Lowie, *The History of Ethnological Theory*, pp. 161-62.

naturally mummified and in many places bodies are embalmed although the practice has nothing to do with religious beliefs. In short, embalming serves a different function. Similar arguments can be made for the differences in form and function where stone idols and tombs are concerned.

In Germany and Austria proponents of the "culture circle" school of diffusion were similarly convinced of the basic uninventiveness of man and the overwhelming importance of borrowing.[7] Their theory and methods, however, were more sophisticated than those of their English counterparts. Where the latter proposed one point of dispersion and relied on single diagnostic traits as proof of contact, the former postulated the independent development and spread of a number of different cultural traditions and used the "culture complex" as evidence of contact. The culture complex consists of a series of interrelated and functionally integrated traits such as a political system, religious ideology, or method of trapping animals, and remains an important concept in contemporary anthropology. Their schemes also included a number of statements regarding *how* culture diffused, that is, notions about the actual processes of change. For example, those complexes found furthest from their hypothetical origin or "hearth" were considered to be the oldest and therefore the earliest to spread; culture traits not functionally related to the fundamental complex (such as the existence of spears in a pacifistic, nohunting society) were assumed to be "secondary developments" derived from contact between two different diffusing traditions; and when two such traditions met head-on they either blended or one was destroyed. Contemporary primitives are not explained by "degeneration," "arrested development," or "dilution" but by the fact that they were pushed into more remote geo-graphical regions by more advanced, encroaching traditions.

Even though based on a broader ethnographic foundation and more rigorous criteria than the pan-Egyptian school, the culture circle proponents provoke similar criticism. Man is still pictured as primarily uninventive, the temporal sequences are denied by archaeological findings, and the fundamental complexes, along with which of these are primary and which are secondary developments, are difficult to establish. Cultural complexity is simply too great to be explained by the interaction of a few traditions emanating from a few hearths. What we have is another grandiose scheme where information is selectively pigeonholed into predetermined categories to substantiate a predetermined theory.

The final school of diffusion, the "American historical school," is not one that was particularly well unified in terms of theory and method. It encompassed rather a series of diverse approaches and interests influenced in one way or another by one scholar—Franz Boas (1858-1942).[8] Boas and his students developed the notion of "culture area" which is defined as the distribution of a particular cultural type and based on the similarity of cultural traits and cultural complexes. In other words, a similar culture occupying a common territory. The culture area concept provided a much-needed scheme for classifying materials in museums and, in addition, allowed *limited* historical recon-

7. For examples of this approach, see, Fritz Graebner, *Methode der Ethnologie* (Heidelberg: C. Winter, 1911) and Wilhelm Schmidt, *The Culture Historical Method of Ethnology* (New York: Fortuny's, Publishers, Inc., 1939).

8. Some of Boas' more important contributions to anthropology can be found in Franz Boas, *Race, Language, and Culture* (New York: The Macmillan Company, 1940).

struction. Boas rejected the sweeping generalizations of the classical evolutionists and the extreme diffusionists. He saw the necessity of considering both independent invention (internal development) and diffusion (external influence) and added a heretofore neglected dimension—environmental influences—which effect both.

The developmental implications of the culture area concept were elaborated by Boas' students and applied in various parts of the world including the two American continents, Africa, and Asia.[9] They proposed that (1) the most dense clustering of similar traits and complexes occurs at the center of the culture area where the most favorable ecological niche for the particular cultural pattern exists (examples from North America would be the northern part of the Northwest where the most abundant salmon and wild game were found, central California where acorns were most prevalent, the Pueblo area of the Southwest where the Hopi and Zuni found the best land for growing maize, and the west central plains where bison were most numerous), (2) the most favorable ecological niche is also the center of the greatest elaboration of the cultural pattern and where the dominant patterns are absorbed, recreated, and radiated outward (this primary source of change is referred to as the culture "climax" or "focus");[10] and finally, (3) those traits and complexes found furthest from the center of dispersal were older and therefore diffused earlier than those closer to the center. This latter proposition is similar to that suggested by the culture circle advocates and has been referred to as the "age-area hypothesis."[11]

Even though this approach is more tempered than previous attempts to explain diffusion and cultural development, some problems are apparent. The theory is based on broad similarities and differences in cultural patterning and pays little atten-

tion to less obvious details, ignores the important principle that the borrowing of traits and complexes is a selective process, and smacks of environmental determinism in equating the most favorable ecological niche with the cultural focus or climax. Further, the latter is difficult to locate. As one critic notes, "a hypothesis that depends on the identification of something and fails to provide a means for its recognition cannot be regarded as helpful. When it also omits detailed definition and avoids analysis, we may perhaps be pardoned for ignoring it."[12] Finally, the assumption that culture diffuses evenly in time and space from a given center takes us back to a unilineal emphasis. Among other factors, geographical barriers such as mountain ranges and bodies of water will influence the direction and rate of diffusion, and traits and complexes may undergo considerable modification once they pass into another environment.[13]

9. For example, see, Clark Wissler, *The Relation of Nature to Man in Aboriginal America* (New York: AMS Press, Inc., 1926); Alfred L. Kroeber, *Configurations of Culture Growth* (Berkeley: University of California Press, 1944); Melville J. Herskovitz, *Cultural Dynamics* (New York: Alfred A. Knopf, Inc., 1947); and Julian H. Steward, ed., *Handbook of South American Indians*, 6 vols. Bureau of American Ethnology Bulletin no. 143 (Washington, D.C., 1946-1950).

10. For more detailed information on the concepts of "culture climax" and "culture focus," see, Alfred L. Kroeber, *Culture Element Distributions III* Publications in American Archaeology and Ethnology, vol. 37, no. 3 (University of California, 1936), pp. 101-16 and Melville J. Herskovitz, *Cultural Dynamics* (New York: Alfred A. Knopf, Inc., 1947).

11. Clark Wissler explained this as "A distribution of narrow range may be suspected of being an innovation, whereas one of wide range would be of respectable age." Wissler, *The Relation of Nature to Man in Aboriginal America*, p. xv.

12. Ian Hogbin, *Social Change* (London: Watts, 1958), p. 95.

13. Roland B. Dixon, *The Building of Cultures* (New York: 1928).

In spite of these drawbacks, however, the contributions of the American school far outweigh their shortcomings. Many of the limited historical reconstructions they proposed are valid, and more importantly perhaps, was Boas' insistence on intensive firsthand field work by a trained investigator working in the native language. By the end of the Boasian period anthropology in the United States is well-grounded in the collection and exhaustive analysis of empirical data, use of the comparative method, and a strong interest in the actual process of change.[14] These emphases are clearly reflected in the burst of acculturation studies which followed and accounted for a large portion of anthropological research in the United States for over two decades.

Boas, however, was not successful in his antievolutionist purge as a new interest in both grand and limited scale cultural evolution occupies a number of American anthropologists from the 1940s on. A brief review of this interest will complete our historical synopsis of the anthropological interest in change.

## NEOEVOLUTION

The renewed interest in evolution was championed by Leslie White (1900-    ) and Julian Steward (1902-1972) and followed by a number of their contemporaries and a generation of their students.[15] The theoretical stance of White and others is similar to that of the classical evolutionists in that they see broad scale trends in the succession of cultural forms everywhere as demonstrable but they do not take the extreme position that every culture everywhere goes through the same unilinear stages. A related axiom held by some, and referred to as "culturology," holds that culture evolves *sui generis* (according to its own laws) thereby relegating the in-

dividual to an insignificant role in the process of culture change.

An example is White's Energy Theory of Cultural Development where he suggests that culture is composed of three subsystems: (1) the technological; (2) the sociological; and (3) the ideological. Social systems and philosophies are functions of technology which is the prime mover in his basic law of cultural evolution. This states that " . . .culture evolves as the amount of energy harnessed per capita per year is increased, or as the efficiency of the instrumental means of putting the energy to work (technology) is increased."[16] Accordingly, White suggests that for the first 990,000 years of human history there was a low per capita output as all energy was derived through the pursuit of hunting and gathering. There followed some minor improvements such as the use of fire to burn out logs for canoes and the invention of the bow and arrow which respectively provided more efficient transportation and hunting techniques. With the development of animal husbandry and agriculture

14. On the continent similar efforts towards making anthropology more scientific were also being made. See, particularly, Bronislaw Malinowski, *Argonauts of the Western Pacific* (London: Routledge and Kegan Paul, Ltd., 1922) and A. R. Radcliffe-Brown, *Structure and Function in Primitive Society* (Glencoe, Ill: The Free Press, 1952).

15. See, for example, V. Gordon Childe, *Man Makes Himself* (New York: Mentor Books, 1951); Alfred A. Kroeber, *The Nature of Culture* (Chicago: The University of Chicago Press, 1952); Marshall D. Sahlins and Elman R. Service, *Evolution and Culture* (Ann Arbor: University of Michigan Press, 1960); Elman R. Service, *Primitive Social Organization: An Evolutionary Perspective* (New York: Random House Inc., 1962); Robert Carniero, "Ascertaining, Testing, and Interpreting Sequences of Cultural Development," *Southwestern Journal of Anthropology* 24 (1969):354-74; and for a general review and bibliography, see, Elman R. Service, *Cultural Evolutionism: Theory and Practice* (New York: Holt, Rinehart and Winston, 1971).

16. Leslie A. White, "The Concept of Culture," *American Anthropologist*, 61(1959), p. 56.

more energy was harnessed from the sun with consequent rapid cultural growth. This process was accelerated even more with the invention of such things as the water wheel, windmill, steam engine, and atomic energy.

An example of the interplay between the three subsystems would be the following: more efficient agricultural production (technology) would free some people from agricultural chores to specialize in such things as government, crafts, and religion. As these specialists gain in power and status a system of inequality expressed in social stratification might develop (sociological). This could then be justified through philosophical notions of inherent social inequality, differential proximity to God, and so on (ideological). Although White's contributions to anthropology are not insignificant,[17] his deification of the culture concept—which leads to the ridiculous premise that culture begets culture—and his use of technology as *the* prime mover is oversimplistic and deterministic. As one of his students has quite correctly pointed out, *"Down with prime movers!* There is no single magical formula that will predict the evolution of every society."[18]

Julian Steward, a contemporary of White, was less gradiose and more tempered in his evolutionary formulations —which prompted White to accuse him of being a historian rather than an anthropologist. Rather than attempting to develop universal laws of cultural development, he searched for significant cross-cultural regularities in cultural change. That is, his theory of Multilinear Evolution was based on the assumption that like causes will produce similar effects even though the cultural settings may be separated in time, space, and lifeways. An example of this can be seen in the comparison of the changes which occurred when fur trappers in Canada and rubber tappers in Brazil were exposed to similar influences induced by contact with the economic practices of white traders.[19]

Prior to contact the Brazilian rubber tappers and Algonkian animal trappers differed in social structure, the general nature of their culture, and adaptation to their respective geographical environments. The tappers were tropical forest hunters and horticulturalists living in semipermanent villages and given to warfare. A strong sense of kinship was reflected in collective hunting, gardening, warfare, and headhunting. Chiefs represented them in trade and led them in war. The trappers, on the other hand, were hunters of large migratory game loosely organized into nomadic bands which often came together in the summer but were not strongly tied one to the other. No definite concept of leadership was established so chieftanship was weak and constantly shifting. Both groups were politically autonomous in that they maintained no larger regional or national ties.

In spite of these and other differences the basic acculturative factors in both cases exerted parallel influences so that the results were similar. Four such factors were common to both tappers and trappers as a result of contact with white traders. First, their involvement in a mercantile

17. See, for example, G. E. Dole and R. L. Carniero, eds., *Essays in the Science of Culture* (In honor of Leslie A. White) (New York: Thomas Y. Crowell, 1960).

18. Service, *Cultural Evolutionism: Theory and Practise*, p. 25.

19. Robert F. Murphy and Julian H. Steward, "Tappers and Trappers: Parallel Process in Acculturation," *Economic Development and Cultural Change*, vol. 4, (July, 1956):335-55. For a general view of Steward's orientation, see, Julian H. Steward, *Theory of Culture Change* (Urbana: University of Illinois Press, 1955) and, for other contributions, see, Robert A. Manners, ed., *Process and Pattern in Culture: Essays in Honor of Julian H. Steward* (Chicago: Aldine Publishing Company, 1964).

barter economy, where their products were traded for supplies, tied them by bonds of debt to the trader who encouraged them to accept more goods than their products were worth. This placed the natives in permanent debt peonage and insured the trader of a constant supply of wild products. Second, collective bonds of kinship and cooperation were undermined as members of each group became increasingly dependent upon the trader. This led to disintegration of traditional bonds and practices which had previously served to integrate and give meaning to the sociocultural system. Third, the dependency on crude latex and animal furs requires a common cultural-ecological adaptation in that both occur in enough quantity in an area most efficiently exploited by one man. Also, both products require careful conservation if productivity is to be maintained. Fourth, the products are sufficiently dispersed to require that persons exploiting them live or work at some distance from one another so that residence patterns had to be altered.

The combination of the effects of these four factors led to similar changes in both groups. Dependency on the trader led to the dissolution of traditional bonds of kinship, cooperation, and authority patterns. The single family became the stable socioeconomic unit with a dispersed settlement pattern generally centered around a trading center. The only permanent bonds beyond the nuclear family were those with the trading centers. This kind of historical construction combined with comparative materials from other studies allows the authors to make limited inferences regarding cultural development. Two are offered in this case:

When goods manufactured by the industrialized nations with modern techniques become available through trade to aboriginal populations, the native people increasingly give up their home crafts in order to devote their efforts to producing specialized cash crops or other trade items in order to obtain more of the industrially made articles. [and] When the people of an unstratified native society barter wild products found in extensive distribution and obtained through individual effort, the structure of the native culture will be destroyed, and the final culmination will be a culture type characterized by individual families having delimited rights to marketable resources and linked to the larger nation through trading centers.[20]

White and Steward carried on an intellectual debate for many years regarding the validity of their respective approaches. Marshall Sahlins has recently attempted to resolve these differences by casting them in a complementary framework. He makes a distinction between *general* and *specific* evolution attributing the former to White and the latter to Steward.

On the one hand, cultural evolution has yielded progressively higher levels of organization: systems exhibiting greater complexity and all-around adaptability. [Sahlins] calls this process or aspect *general evolution*. On the other hand, as new cultural types emerge, they undergo an inevitable process of radiation and adaptation to their specific total environments. Consequently, he refers to this process or aspect as *specific evolution*.[21]

In short, Sahlins suggests that White's concern with long-term evolutionary development does not conflict with Steward's search for more specific instances of adaptive regularities within the broader spectrum of evolutionary change. Regard-

20. Murphy and Steward, "Tappers and Trappers: Parallel Process in Acculturation," p. 353.

21. David Kaplan and Robert A. Manners, *Culture Theory* (Englewood Cliffs, New Jersey: Prentice-Hall, Inc., 1972), pp. 48-49.

less, both men and their followers have played a significant role in the development of the change literature and their ideas continue to exert considerable influence.

## SUMMARY

Anthropology was born with a consuming interest in unraveling the mysteries of man's past. In their search for answers to these mysteries early anthropologists were forced to rely on secondhand accounts of other peoples and other places provided primarily by explorers, traders, colonial officers, and missionaries. The classical evolutionists used this sketchy data base to theorize that culture everywhere developed according to the same unilineal scheme because man's mental processes were universally the same. The extreme diffusionists denied man's inventiveness and instead based their schemes on broad scale borrowing as culture diffused from one or several hearths to the rest of the world. Franz Boas and his students rejected these grandiose formulations based on "armchair theorizing" and insisted on systematically collected, firsthand information to establish their limited historical reconstructions. A renewed interest in broad scale evolutionary trends is reflected in neoevolutionism although the proponents of this school are more reasonable in their approach and have the advantage of an empirical data base. Acculturation and directed change became important areas of concern for the anthropologist in the mid-twentieth century. More recently, an interest in the changes occurring as underdeveloped countries are drawn into the mainstream of more modern ways has occupied the interests of an increasing number of anthropologists. We will treat these topics in some detail after a consideration of how and why change occurs.

## For Further Reading

Boas, F. *Race, Language, and Culture*. New York: The Macmillan Company, 1940. A number of essays by Franz Boas which serve to clarify his basic theoretical, methodological, and substantive interests. Many ideas are presented which antedate some areas of current thinking in anthropology.

Harris, M. *The Rise of Anthropological Theory*. New York: Thomas Y. Crowell Company, 1968. A contemporary but biased account of the history of anthropology with emphasis on current theoretical issues.

Hays, H. R. *From Ape to Angel: An Informal History of Social Anthropology*. New York: Alfred A. Knopf, 1958. A well-written and readable account of the history of anthropology for laymen and professionals alike.

Lowie, R. H. *The History of Ethnological Theory*. New York: Holt, Rinehart and Winston, 1937. A classic scholarly critique of early anthropologists and their works.

Penniman, T. K. *One Hundred Years of Anthropology*. Cambridge: Harvard University Press, 1936. A fascinating account of early anthropology emphasizing the growth of archaeology. Complete with intrigue, professional competition, and grave-robbers. Fun reading.

Sahlins, M. D. and E. R. Service, eds. *Evolution and Culture*. Ann Arbor: University of Michigan Press, 1960. A series of essays prepared primarily by students of Leslie White and Julian Steward which serve to define the neo-evolutionary position.

## Bibliography

Boas, F. 1940. *Race, Language, and Culture*. New York: The Macmillan Company.

Carniero, R. 1969. "Ascertaining, Testing, and Interpreting Sequences of Cultural Development," *Southwestern Journal of Anthropology* 24: 354-374.

Childe, V. G. 1951. *Man Makes Himself.* New York: Mentor Books.

Dixon, R. B. 1928. *The Building of Cultures.* New York.

Dole, G. E. and Carniero, R. L. eds. 1960. *Essays in the Science of Culture* (in honor of Leslie A. White). New York: Thomas Y. Crowell Company.

Graebner, F. 1911. *Methode der Ethnologie.* Heidelberg: C. Winter.

Hays, H. R. 1958. *From Ape to Angel: An Informal History of Social Anthropology.* New York: Alfred A. Knopf.

Herskovitz, M. J. 1947. *Cultural Dynamics.* New York: Alfred A. Knopf.

Hogbin, I. 1958. *Social Change.* London: Watts.

Kaplan D. and Manners, R. R. 1972. *Culture Theory.* Englewood Cliffs, N.J.: Prentice-Hall, Inc.

Kroeber, A. L. 1936. "Culture Element Distributions III," Publications in American Archaeology and Ethnology, vol. 37, no. 3. University of California.

———. 1944. *Configurations of Culture Growth.* Berkeley: University of California Press.

Kroeber, A. L. and Kluckhohn, C. 1952. *The Nature of Culture.* Chicago: University of Chicago Press.

Lowie, R. H. 1937. *The History of Ethnological Theory.* New York: Holt, Rinehart, and Winston.

Malinowski, B. 1922. *Argonauts of the Western Pacific.* London: Routledge and Kegan Paul Ltd.

Manners, R. A., ed. 1964. *Process and Pattern in Culture: Essays in Honor of Julian H. Steward.* Chicago: Aldine Publishing Company.

Morgan, L. H. 1877. *Ancient Society.* New York: Henry Holt and Company.

Murphy, R. F. and Steward, J. H. 1956. "Tappers and Trappers: Parallel Process in Acculturation." *Economic Development and Cultural Change* 4: 335-355.

Perry, W. J. 1923. *The Children of the Sun.* London: Metheuw and Company.

Radcliffe-Brown, A. R. 1952. *Structure and Function in Primitive Society.* Glencoe, Ill.: The Free Press.

Sahlins, M. D. and Service, E. R. eds. 1960. *Evolution and Culture.* Ann Arbor: The University of Michigan Press.

Schmidt, W. 1939. *The Culture Historical Method of Ethnology.* New York: Fortuny's Publishers Inc.

Service, E. R. 1962. *Primitive Social Organization: An Evolutionary Perspective.* New York: Random House, Inc.

———. 1971. *Cultural Evolutionism: Theory and Practice.* New York: Holt, Rinehart, and Winston.

Smith, G. E. 1928. *In the Beginning: The Origin of Civilization.* London: G. Howe, Ltd.

Steward, J. H., ed. 1946-1950. *Handbook of South American Indians,* vol. 1-6. Washington, D.C.: Bureau of American Ethnology. Bulletin 143.

———. 1955. *Theory of Culture Change.* Urbana: University of Illinois Press.

Tylor, E. B. 1871. *Primitive Culture: Researches into the Development of Mythology, Religion, Language, Art, and Custom.* Boston: Estes and Lauriat.

White, L. A. 1959. "The Concept of Culture." *American Anthropologist* 61: 227-251.

Wissler, C. 1926. *The Relation of Nature to Man in Aboriginal America.* New York: AMS Press, Inc.

# 2 | The Process of Change

In the introduction it was stated that change is a constant in all sociocultural systems even though the rate of change and the form it manifests vary greatly from one situation to the next. In this section we will discuss the actual process of change. That is, *why* and *how* does culture change?

In the framework to be presented, change generally follows modification in either the sociocultural or physical environment. Often changes in both occur simultaneously or follow one another. As used here, the sociocultural environment refers to man, culture, and society where the physical environment refers to a particular ecological setting, both natural—such as mountains and plains and man-made—such as buildings and roads. Examples of modifications in the sociocultural environment might be an increase in population density, contact with other peoples, or the advent of a new political system; while migration to a new area, natural catastrophes, and climatic changes would represent modifications in the physical environment. An example of both would be movement from rural to urban areas where both the sociocultural and physical environments would require new responses. In any case, when an environmental modification favors new patterns of thought and behavior, the prerequisites of sociocultural change are present.

## INNOVATION

In a classic work devoted to understanding the process of change Homer Barnett established once and for all that innovation is the basis of all culture change. He defines an innovation as

...any thought, behavior, or thing that is new because qualitatively different from existing forms...every innovation is an idea or a constellation of ideas; but some innovations by their nature must remain mental organization only, whereas others may be given overt and tangible expression.[1]

In this sense, change begins when *individual* members of a given society respond in novel ways to environmental modifications. By definition, however, actual culture change does not occur until the new response is learned and accepted by sufficient numbers of people so that it becomes characteristic of the group.

Students of change commonly recognize four basic variants of innovation: (1) long-term variation, (2) discovery, (3) invention, and (4) diffusion, or borrowing. *Long-term variation* refers to the gradual

1. Homer G. Barnett, *Innovation: The Basis of Cultural Change* (New York: McGraw-Hill Book Company, 1953), p. 7.

accumulation of slight modifications in existing patterns of thought and behavior over time resulting in something qualitatively new. The individual increments of change may be slight but their cumulative effect over extended periods of time may be considerable. Examples might be slowly increasing ceremonial elaboration, the growth of complexity in social organization, or the gradual increase of scientific knowledge. The term evolution is appropriate to refer to such changes.

*Discovery* is the act of becoming aware of something which has been in existence but not previously perceived where *invention* is a new synthesis of preexistent materials, conditions, or practices. The distinction is not always an easy one to follow although, in general, discovering is "finding" and inventing is "making."[2] The bow and arrow, various religious ideologies, and the automobile were inventions while fire, natural vitamins, and the principles of biological evolution were discoveries. Some students of change further dichotomize both discovery and invention into accidental and volitional, and inventions, into basic and secondary.[3] While these distinctions may be conceptually useful in some cases they commonly involve hair-splitting and will not be further discussed here.

One facet of invention that does merit attention is *accidental juxtaposition* since it probably played a very significant role in the early stages of cultural development. This has been defined as

the creation of a new implement as the sequel to the establishment of a close spatial relationship between two or more objects, or of a close temporal relationship between the mental images of two or more objects, by natural or artifical means without foreknowledge of the result.[4]

More simply stated this concept implies that two or more previously unrelated

ideas or objects are brought together so that something new is created. For example, the discovery of charred animals burned in a forest fire may have led to the practice of cooking and a log being carried downstream with a bird perched upon it may have given man the idea for the invention of the canoe.

The advent of bullfighting can be attributed to accidental juxtaposition. The noblemen in Andalusian Spain at one time killed wild bulls from horseback to keep their war skills sharp, inspire their peers to valor, and provide a spectacle for the lesser born. On one such occasion at the beginning of the eighteenth century a nobleman was upended and pinned underneath his steed, helpless before the horns of the bull he had intended to kill.

As the bull poised to drive those horns into the nobleman's body, one of the village poor, hired to tend the Royal Riding Circle, leaped into the ring. Using his flat-brimmed Andalusian hat as a lure, he drew the bull away from the helpless rider. Then, to the awe and admiration of his noble employers, he continued to wave his hat before the bull's eyes, and fixing the beast's stare to its movements, he lured the horned animal past his body time and time again.[5]

Thus it was, that Francisco Romero, a carpenter's assistant, founded the ritual of the modern bullfight—a conflict between a bull, a dismounted man, and the lure of a fluttering piece of cloth.

As in accidental juxtaposition both dis-

2. Bryce F. Ryan, *Social and Cultural Change* (New York: The Ronald Press Company, 1969), p. 78.

3. Barnett, *Innovation: The Basis of Cultural Change*, chap. 7.

4. E. F. Greenman, "Material Culture and the Organism," *American Anthropologist* 47 (1945): 215.

5. Larry Collins and Dominique Lapierre, *Or I'll Dress You in Mourning* (New York: Signet Books, 1968), p. xi.

covery and invention involve a *mental* act which requires that one or more existing things be conceptually broken into *parts* and that one or some of these parts be modified, replaced, or recombined so that a *new* structure exists. As we have shown above, however, they do differ. Significantly, an invention can be patented while a discovery cannot.[6] A few more observations about discovery and invention are in order. First, since both are dependent upon the existing cultural inventory, the process proceeds more rapidly in groups with a greater complexity of social and cultural forms. Second, the latter implies that change has a "snowballing" effect in that modification leads to greater complexity and greater complexity leads to further and more accelerated changes. Third, where similar cultural inventories exist the probability of independent invention is greater. In short, when the elements of an appropriate synthesis are present, someone will carry it out. Common examples include the development of agriculture in both Asia and America, the independent formulations of the theory of natural selection by Charles Darwin and Alfred Wallace, and the receipt of patent applications for the telephone by Bell and Gray on the same day.

### DIFFUSION

No contemporary scholar of change would disagree that *diffusion,* or borrowing, is the most common form of innovation. From this it follows that the overwhelming majority of items in the cultural inventory are borrowed—particularly where more modern societies are concerned. Ralph Linton has offered a humorous illustration of this where American culture is concerned.

Our solid American citizen awakens in a bed built on a pattern which originated in the Near East but which was modified in Northern Europe before it was transmitted to America. He throws back covers made from cotton, domesticated in India, or linen, domesticated in the Near East, or wool from sheep, also domesticated in the Near East, or silk, the use of which was discovered in China. All of these materials have been spun and woven by processes invented in the Near East. He slips into his moccasins, invented by the Indians of the Eastern woodlands, and goes to the bathroom, whose fixtures are a mixture of European and American inventions, both of recent date. He takes off his pajamas, a garment invented in India, and washes with soap invented by the ancient Gauls. He then shaves, a masochistic rite which seems to have been derived from either Sumer or ancient Egypt.

Returning to the bedroom, he removes his clothes from a chair of southern European type and proceeds to dress. He puts on garments whose form originally derived from the skin clothing of the nomads of the Asiatic steppes, puts on shoes made from skins tanned by a process invented in ancient Egypt and cut to a pattern derived from the classical civilizations of the Mediterranean, and ties around his neck a strip of bright-colored cloth which is a vestigial survival of the shoulder shawls worn by the seventeenth-century Croatians. Before going out for breakfast he glances through the window, made of glass invented in Egypt, and if it is raining puts on overshoes made of rubber discovered by the Central American Indians and takes an umbrella, invented in southeastern Asia. Upon his head he puts a hat made of felt, a material invented in the Asiatic steppes.

On his way to breakfast he stops to buy a paper, paying for it with coins, an ancient Lydian invention. At the restaurant a whole new series of borrowed elements confronts him. His plate is made of a form of pottery invented in China. His knife is of steel, an alloy first made in southern India, his fork a medie-

6. E. Adamson Hoebel, *Anthropology: The Study of Man,* 4th ed. (New York: McGraw-Hill Book Company, 1972), p. 646.

val Italian invention, and his spoon a derivative of a Roman original. He begins breakfast with an orange, from the eastern Mediterranean, a canteloupe from Persia, or perhaps a piece of African watermelon. With this he has coffee, an Abyssinian plant, with cream and sugar. Both the domestication of cows and the idea of milking them originated in the Near East, while sugar was first made in India. After his fruit and first coffee he goes on to waffles, cakes made by a Scandinavian technique from wheat domesticated in Asia Minor. Over these he pours syrup, invented by the Indians of the Eastern Woodlands. As a side dish he may have the egg of a species of bird domesticated in Indo-China, or thin strips of flesh of an animal domesticated in Eastern Asia which may have been salted and smoked by a process developed in northern Europe.

When our friend has finished eating he settles back to smoke, an American habit, consuming a plant domesticated in Brazil in either a pipe, derived from the Indians of Virginia, or a cigarette, derived from Mexico. If he is hardy enough he may even attempt a cigar, transmitted to us from the Antilles by way of Spain. While smoking he reads the news of the day, imprinted in characters invented by the ancient Semites upon a material invented in China by a process invented in Germany. As he absorbs the accounts of foreign troubles he will, if he is a good conservative citizen, thank a Hebrew deity in an Indo-European language that he is 100 percent American.[7]

This is a somewhat dramatic example of how many traits of different origins can end up in one place. The diffusion of tobacco illustrates the other side of the coin—the many different places in which a single trait can end up.

Tobacco was discovered in the New World. It was introduced into Spain in 1558 as a medicine and into the English court by Sir Walter Raleigh around 1586. It diffused throughout the Old World from these two points of dispersion. Smoking travelled to Holland via English medical students in 1590 and spread by sea into the Baltic and Scandinavian countries and then overland through Germany into Russia where legislation was enacted against it in 1634. In the next 200 years it crossed the steppes and mountains of Siberia and was reintroduced to North America across the Bering Straits into Alaska—through the back door so to speak. Tobacco diffused from Spain and Portugal through the Mediterranean countries, to Africa, South America, and the Far East. Turkey passed laws against its use in 1605 and in the same year Japan placed restrictions on its cultivation.

As tobacco diffused, so did the forms of its use. The North American Indians smoked it in pipes as did the English and those who picked it up from them. The Indians of Brazil preferred cigars and the Mexicans passed cigarettes on to their Spanish conquerers who then carried them to Turkey and Egypt. Both pipe and cigar entered Southeast Asia and the pipe took hold in Africa. The water pipe, which only recently entered the United States, originated in the Near East and snuff spread from Spain to the French court and to other European nobility. Cigarette smoking was picked up by the English from their Turkish allies during the Crimean War but not brought into the United States until after 1850 where it met with considerable opposition.[8]

A special kind of diffusion occurs when the idea for a trait or complex is borrowed but the actual content is not. In this kind of situation, referred to as "stimulus diffusion,"[9] it remains for the receiving culture to develop the content proposed by the idea. A hypothetical example would be

7. Ralph Linton, *The Study of Man: An Introduction* (New York: Appleton-Century-Crofts, Inc., 1936), pp. 326-27.

8. Ibid., pp. 331-33.

9. Alfred L. Kroeber, "Stimulus Diffusion," *American Anthropologist* 42 (1940):1-20.

where a member of one group without the canoe visits a group with this vessel and takes the idea home with him. He has the concept but then must find materials, develop means for actual construction and use, and incorporate all this into the cultural inventory. Most examples of stimulus diffusion in the literature involve borrowing the idea of a written language by various groups who have then devised their own unique syllabary and phonetics.

## A MODEL OF CHANGE

Our discussion regarding the general process of change to this point can be diagramatically summarized as shown in Figure A. Modification in the sociocultural or physical environment favors new responses as individuals adapt to changing circumstances. Innovation is the source of these adaptations and takes the form of long-term variation, discovery, invention, and diffusion. Actual sociocultural change occurs when a plurality of the group learns and accepts the new response so that it becomes part of shared, habitual patterns of behavior.

But note that our model is not a unilinear one. This is indicated by the arrows proceeding in both directions. The process of change can begin at either end and interplay among the components is common.

For example, the diffusion of improved medical practices to underdeveloped countries (an innovation) can lead to dangerously high population levels (an environmental modification) which can then create the need to consciously seek efficient means of population control (innovations).

### SUMMARY

A general model of the change process was outlined in this chapter. This is based on the principle that innovation is the basis of all cultural change. Four basic variants of innovation were discussed and the overwhelming importance of one of these variants, diffusion, was underlined. This is clearly reflected in the various examples given. One of these showed how many elements of foreign origin confront the 100 percent American on an average morning and another traces the diffusion of tobacco from North America around the world and back again. Because of the importance of diffusion in culture change, the succeeding chapter is devoted to a more detailed consideration of its characteristics.

### For Further Reading

Barnett, H. G. *Innovation: The Basis of Cultural Change*. New York: McGraw-Hill, 1953.

## FIGURE A

### GENERALIZED MODEL OF THE CHANGE PROCESS

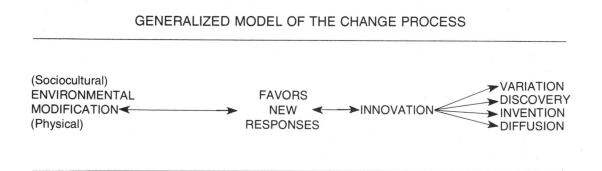

This book presents Barnett's classic exposition of the importance of innovation in all culture change. He also discusses the characteristics of innovators, examines acceptance and rejection, and presents a wealth of descriptive material.

Etzioni, A. and E. Etzioni, eds. *Social Change: Sources, Patterns, and Consequences.* New York: Basic Books, Inc., 1964. One of the better collections of basic readings on change. A number of classic essays are included.

Linton, R. *The Study of Man.* New York: Appleton-Century-Crofts, 1936. This is undoubtedly one of the best books ever written in anthropology and herein lie the seeds of many issues of contemporary import. Where change is concerned most of the basic processes are discussed and the volume is laced with rich and original examples.

Mead, M., ed. *Cultural Patterns and Technical Change.* Paris: UNESCO, 1953. Mead attempts to show that by relating changes to existing community values, Western technology and science can be used to enhance rather than destroy traditional patterns of living.

Pelto, P. J. *The Snowmobile Revolution: Technology and Social Change in the Arctic.* Menlo Park, California: Cummings Publishing Company, 1973. The snowmobile was introduced to the reindeer-herding Skolts in northeastern Finland in the early 1960s. Pelto shows how this technological innovation set off a series of linked changes which eventually effected almost every aspect of Skolt life. Very well done and highly recommended.

Ryan, B. F. *Social and Cultural Change.* New York: The Ronald Press, 1969. An introduction to the sociology of change which includes considerable anthropological materials. Read selectively.

### Bibliography

Barnett, H. G. 1953. *Innovation: The Basis of Cultural Change.* New York: McGraw-Hill Book Company.

Collins, L. and Lapierre, D. 1968. *Or I'll Dress You in Mourning.* New York: Signet Books.

Greenman, E. F. 1945. "Material Culture and the Organism," *American Anthropologist* 47: 212-231.

Hoebel, E. A. 1972. *Anthropology: The Study of Man* 4th ed. New York: McGraw Hill Book Company.

Kroeber, A. L. 1940. "Stimulus Diffusion." *American Anthropologist* 42: 1-20.

Linton, R. 1936. *The Study of Man: An Introduction.* New York: Appleton-Century-Crofts, Inc.

Ryan, B. F. 1969. *Social and Cultural Change.* New York: The Ronald Press.

# 3 | The Process of Diffusion

Since diffusion, or borrowing, is such an important variant of innovation it warrants more detailed consideration. Research has shown that even though the process of borrowing varies greatly from place to place and situation to situation, certain regularities can be isolated. Still, because of the variability which always accompanies change, even these broad generalizations must be taken with caution.

### BASIC CHARACTERISTICS

First of all, *borrowing is selective.* People do not accept everything that is offered or available in the cultural inventory of the group or groups with which they come into contact. In general, traits are accepted or rejected on the bais of their utility, compatibility, and meaning in the receiving culture. A trait must have utility for the potential borrowers to be adopted. Thus the acceptance of a tractor in rocky, hillside farming regions or of "Hamburger Helper" among Hindus (who consider cattle sacred) would be unlikely. Similarly, the acceptance of contraceptives in Catholic countries, or abortion in declining populations, is unlikely due to lack of compatibility, or fit, with existing patterns. Hari Kari would not be borrowed by Americans because it is contrary to religious teachings and because Americans

do not adhere to the concept of "face" in such drastic form.[1] There would be a lack of mental fit, or meaning.

Closely related to the concept of selective borrowing is the notion that *some innovations are adopted more rapidly than others.* In an extensive review of the diffusion literature Everett Rogers concluded that the rate of adoption of a given innovation is effected by its relative advantage, compatibility, complexity, trialability, and observability in the receiving culture.[2] *Relative advantage* refers to the degree to which an innovation is perceived as superior to the trait it replaces. *Compatibility*, as noted above, is the degree to which the innovation is perceived as consistent with existing values, experience, and needs. *Complexity* is the degree to which an innovation is perceived as difficult to understand and use, and *trialability* the extent to which the innovation can be experimented with on a limited basis. The degree to which positive results of an innovation can be seen by others refers to its *observability*. In sum, Rogers suggests that the rate of adoption for a given innovation is

1. Lowell D. Holmes, *Anthropology: An Introduction* (New York: The Ronald Press Company, 1965), p. 285.
2. Everett M. Rogers with F. F. Shoemaker, *Communication of Innovations: A Cross-Cultural Approach* (New York: The Free Press, 1971), pp. 22-23.

proportionate to the degree to which it is seen as superior to that which it is to supercede, consistent with existing patterns, easy to comprehend and apply, capable of being tried on a limited basis, and visible to others. The negation of these principles should tend to slow down, if not prohibit altogether, the acceptance of a particular innovation.

It is also true that *some people adopt innovations sooner than others.* Once an innovation is made available to a particular group the process of adoption proceeds from individual to individual. And because different people have varying motivations, values, vested interests, and predispositions to change, some will adopt the new practice sooner than others. Again, based on his review of the diffusion literature, Rogers has proposed a series of ideal adopter categories which he likens to a normal curve. These categories are shown in Figure B. The *innovators* are those who first adopt a new practice. Rogers describes them as venturesome individuals who have a high degree of exposure to the outside world, control of considerable financial resources, are willing to take risks, and have the ability to understand complex technical knowledge. *Early*

*adopters* are respected individuals who have greater vested interests in the local cultural tradition than innovators. Others in the community will look to these leaders for advice before accepting a new practice. The *early majority* are less likely to hold positions of leadership and will ponder carefully the consequences of adoption prior to taking action. Where the early majority will adopt just prior to the average member of the social system, the *late majority* adopt just after the average member. They are skeptical people and peer pressure is necessary for them to go along with the rest of society. *Laggards* are the more traditional members of the group who tend to be suspicious of any kind of change. They are openly conservative and prefer the status quo.

It should be emphasized that these adopter categories are ideal rather than real and are constructed for purposes of demonstration and comparison. Grouping people into these categories allows generalization. The actual process is more closely akin to a continuum as adoption progresses

3. Adapted from Rogers with Shoemaker, *Communication of Innovations: A Cross-Cultural Approach,* p. 182.

## FIGURE B
### ADOPTER CATEGORIES APPROXIMATING A NORMAL CURVE[3]

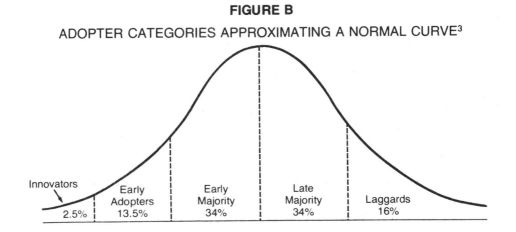

| Innovators | Early Adopters | Early Majority | Late Majority | Laggards |
|:---:|:---:|:---:|:---:|:---:|
| 2.5% | 13.5% | 34% | 34% | 16% |

through the society. In addition, Rogers' work is based primarily on studies of the introduction of one or a few traits from Western technology into Western society or into Third World societies. As such, his findings may not be as valid where contact is more intense and where more primitive groups are concerned.

Nevertheless his generalizations regarding adopters are worthy of note. As opposed to later adopters, early adopters are (1) better educated, (2) more literate, (3) of higher social status, (4) more upwardly mobile, (5) involved in larger, commercially oriented, and specialized operations, and (6) more favorably disposed to credit negotiations. In addition, age was found to be irrelevant where early or late adoption was concerned.[4] Some of these propositions will be further discussed in proceeding chapters.

*The extent of borrowing is largely dependent on the duration and intensity of contact* between the two groups. Peoples who are in continuous firsthand contact are more likely to borrow from one another than those where contact is sporadic. The many different ethnic and cultural groups who emigrated to the United States found themselves in what has been described as a "melting pot" where individual and group differences gave way to common understandings and patterns of behavior. This process, whereby two or more previously separated cultural traditions combine to produce new patterns is commonly referred to as *assimilation*. Some of these migrants to the United States though, had less contact with the others and retained many of their native customs. To this day some remain marginal to the mainstream of American life.

In Middle America the assimilation of Spanish and native American cultures into a combination of selected aspects of both has been referred to as "conquest culture" because Spanish ways were initially forced on the Indians and tend to predominate.[5] Still, while most Indian groups have been hispanicized to the point where they can no longer remember their formal tribal affiliations, there remain groups who have been relatively isolated because of geographical and/or sociopolitical reasons who retain many of their traditional beliefs and practices. They have been less exposed to the forces of assimilation. This is particularly true for groups in the southeastern highlands of Mexico and throughout highland Guatemala.

Contact does not, however, always result in drastic changes in one or both groups. Literature on the subject affords examples of close contact with relatively little borrowing such as the Todas and English in India, the Reindeer Tungus and Cossacks in northwestern Manchuria, and, to some extent, the Pygmies and Bantu in the African Congo.[6] The latter case shows both selective borrowing and the importance of the contact situation. The Bantu live in sedentary villages on the edge of the forest. Basically agriculturalists, they rely on the Pygmies, who live in the forest and practice hunting and gathering, for meat. In return they supply the Pygmies with some agricultural produce and perform initiation ceremonies for young pygmy males. Apart from this limited symbiotic relationship, both groups retain their separate cultural traditions. Attempts to locate the Pygmies in sedentary villages have

---

4. Ibid., pp. 185-86.

5. George M. Foster, *Culture and Conquest: America's Spanish Heritage* (Viking Fund Publications in Anthropology, no. 27), 1960.

6. See, David G. Mandelbaum, "Culture Change Among the Nilgiri Tribes," *American Anthropologist* 43 (1941):19-26; E. J. Lindgren, "An Example of Culture Contact Without Conflict: Reindeer Tungus and Cossacks in Northwestern Manchuria," *American Anthropologist* 40 (1938):605-62; and Colin Turnbull, *The Forest People* (New York: Doubleday, 1962).

largely failed. They prefer the forest which they see as benevolent and the provider of all good things. The Bantu, on the other hand, see only evil in the forest and prefer their village life. And, even though the Pygmies have borrowed the initiation rites of the Bantu, they have not accepted related witchcraft beliefs and practices.[7]

It has also been shown that *borrowing is more likely in a system which is "off balance"* than one which is well integrated.[8] No society is perfectly integrated in the sense that it provides a satisfactory way of life for the whole population. There are always discontented, maladjusted, or otherwise "deviant" people about. If this element in a given society reaches sufficient strength and numbers they may well challenge the status quo. Such a society, where large numbers of the population are already seeking alternative ways, is more susceptible to change than one where satisfaction, or apathy, is the rule. It was such a situation which led the "founding fathers" of the United States to draft a new government based on different ideas from a number of established European governments. Similarly, many Indian groups in preconquest Mexico were dissatisfied with the oppression of their Aztec rulers and openly sided with the Spanish invaders to topple them from power.

Contact itself, of course, can lead to cultural disintegration. This is particularly true when one group dominates another as in a conquest situation. Stripped of many of their social, political, and religious institutions, the Indians of Middle America readily adopted those of the conquering Spaniards. Where religion was concerned they managed to adapt many of their pagan beliefs and practices into the structure of Catholicism. This blending of traits from separate traditions into something qualitatively new is referred to as a *syncretism*. This particular syncretism was greatly aided by the basic similarity between the two religious systems.

This leads to another feature of diffusion: *borrowing is greater among groups with similar cultural inventories*. The extent and rate of borrowing is affected by the degree to which the groups in contact share common cultural meaning and content. This follows logically from the premise that traits and complexes from similar groups are more likely to "fit" and that certain features are prerequisite to others. The complex technology of Western society cannot be borrowed by groups who cannot manufacture such things as steel or muster huge amounts of power, a miniskirt would make little sense to people who have no concept of clothing, and bison-hunting Plains Indians would have had little use for the rabbit hunting techniques of their Shoshone neighbors to the north or the agricultural practices of the Hopi and Zuni to the south.

Even though one group may dominate another, *borrowing commonly proceeds in both directions*. The process of diffusion is not a unidirectional affair where one group gives and the other receives. It is, rather, a two-way street where both groups in contact selectively adopt traits and complexes from one another. This interchange can be illustrated with an example concerning native Americans and the white man.

The white man brought the horse but borrowed the canoe; while many American Indians today live in European style houses, many Americans spend at least their two weeks vacation in a tent. American Indian Jim Thorpe was a nationally known All-American and pro-football player, while many an Ivy League college student plays on a varsity lacrosse team. In the area of foodstuffs, the white man got somewhat the better of the deal. He borrowed corn, beans, squash,

7. Turnbull, *The Forest People.*
8. Max Gluckman, "Analysis of a Social Situation in Modern Zululand," *Bantu Studies*, no. 2, 14 (1940):135.

hominy, popcorn, wild rice, melons, cocoa, tomatoes, pumpkin, potatoes, and turkeys.[9]

As previously noted, we also borrowed tobacco from the North American Indians and the practice of smoking it in cigarettes from the Mexicans. In contemporary Guatemala tourists are literally buying native costumes off the Indians' backs. On the other hand, many of these Indians, though they still live in houses of mud and straw and cook on an open fire between three stones on the floor, have acquired transistor radios, modern clothing, wristwatches, and numerous other elements of Western technology. Recently these Mayan Indians have begun to use small outboard motors to propel their canoes which are still hewn from a single tree trunk.

Reciprocal borrowing also reflects the fact that, in general, as underdeveloped groups begin to acquire the rudiments of a more modern way of life, *they are exposed to a bundle of technological items* at the same time rather than single traits. Thus it is difficult to discuss the effects of the introduction of something like modern medicine without also considering those of other innovations ordinarily introduced at the same time. These might include, for example, literacy programs, agricultural cooperatives, religious proselytizing, exposure to the mass media, and any number of other items and ideas from Western technology and culture.

*Reinterpretation* is another characteristic of diffusion. Seldom are traits and complexes transferred in exactly their original configuration. Usually they undergo alterations in form, function, and/or meaning in order to fit the particular needs of the receiving culture. We have already seen this principle in operation with assimilation and syncretism. By way of review, assimilation refers to the blending of separate cultural traditions into a qualitatively new tradition where syncretism is the blending of single traits or complexes rather than whole traditions. Reinterpretation is the general process whereby these new syntheses take place. E. Adamson Hoebel has offered a particularly illuminating example of this as the sun dance was adopted and reinterpreted by various North American Indian groups.

The sun dance was a complex ceremony which spread from the Arapaho and Cheyenne to other tribes in the Western Plains. In its fundamental core the dance was universal but it was reinterpreted in form, function, and meaning as it diffused from one group to the other. Among the Shoshone and Utes it was stripped of its military overtones since these groups were basically pacifistic and lacked military fraternities. Instead, they used it as a purification and curing ceremony. For the highly militaristic Crow, the sun dance was a prelude to a war party and for the Cheyenne it remained a world-renewal ceremony. The Commanches used it once in an effort to make them immune from bullets but were consequently defeated badly in warfare and did not try it again —the ritual failed to provide function or meaning for them. Currently the sun dance is performed on various reservations to reinforce tribal integrity in an attempt to ease the effect of disintegrative forces brought about by contact with the non-Indian world.[10]

All students of change would agree that *some parts of the cultural inventory are more resistant to change than others* although there is considerable debate regarding which parts are most resistant to change. In anthropology there is a strong tradition which argues that changes in behavior precede changes in belief. This was evident in White's Energy Theory of Cul-

9. Holmes, *Anthropology: An Introduction,* p. 291.
10. E. Adamson Hoebel, *Anthropology: The Study of Man,* 4th ed. (New York: McGraw-Hill Book Company, 1972), pp. 653-54.

tural Development where technological changes precede modifications in the sociological and ideological spheres. Similarly, this writer has shown that changes in medical behavior, such as use of the doctor over the shaman, precede changes in medical beliefs which support use of the shaman, in a Guatemalan community. Felix Keesing has argued in a similar vein suggesting that essentials of psychosomatic conditioning, communication, organic maintenance, primary group relations, prestige status maintenance, and territorial and ideological security are most resistant to change while such things as tools, etiquette, military techniques, elements of taste and expression, achieved status systems, competitive types of behavior, and impersonal or mass social structures are more susceptible to modification and therefore are more likely to change first.[11] Others have suggested that regardless of what sets off the process, central value orientations provide a crucial guideline for the direction of change.[12]

By contrast, a competing theoretical viewpoint emanating primarily from sociology argues that ideological systems are more fundamental, either inhibiting or predisposing the process of change. Thus Max Weber asserted that an inherent Protestant ethic led to the development of capitalism in Europe and the United States, Everett Hagen sees personality change as providing a predisposition to social upheaval and revolution in the underdeveloped countries, and Wilbert Moore maintains that aesthetic forms and supernatural beliefs, because they are relatively autonomous of other elements in the social system, can change independently of other parts.[13] We will address these issues further in later sections.

In psychological anthropology Edward Bruner has proposed that the earlier something is learned, the more difficult it is to change.[14] He holds that the products of

child conditioning such as language, facial expressions, moral and ethical standards, basic food preferences, and basic motor habits change more slowly than traits acquired as adults. An example of this is afforded by Margaret Mead's work with the Manus in the South Pacific.[15] In her early work she found that children were taught to be independent, alert, and resourceful. Later in life young adults were taught a variety of strict taboos and avoidances along with an extremely puritanical sex code. When Mead returned to the Manus about twenty-five years later she found that contact with Western ways had resulted in changes in adult patterns in accordance with Western values but that patterns learned in childhood remained resistant to change.

These divergent theoretical views serve to document the fact that the process of change is an extremely complicated one. The what, how, and why of change will vary from situation to situation depending on a number of different circumstances. This is one reason for the lack of good change theory in the anthropological liter-

11. Felix M. Keesing, *Culture Change: An Analysis and Bibliography of Anthropological Sources to 1952* (Stanford: Stanford University Press, 1952), p. 83.

12. Evon Z. Vogt, "On the Concepts of Structure and Process in Cultural Anthropology," *American Anthropologist* 62 (1960):18-33.

13. For further elaboration refer to Max Weber, *The Protestant Ethic and the Spirit of Capitalism* (New York: Charles Scribner and Sons, 1953); Everette E. Hagen, *On the Theory of Social Change* (Homewood, Illinois: The Dorsey Press, 1962); and Wilbert E. Moore, *Social Change* (Englewood Cliffs, New Jersey: Prentice-Hall, 1963).

14. Edward M. Bruner, "Cultural Transmission and Culture Change," *Southwestern Journal of Anthropology* 12 (1956):191-99.

15. See, especially, Margaret Mead, *Coming of Age in Samoa* (New York: William Morrow and Company, 1928) and idem, *New Lives For Old: Cultural Transformation-Manus, 1928-1953* (New York: William Morrow and Company, 1956).

ature. We will come back to this, but for the moment simply state that there is no one theory which can account for the many intricacies of the process of change.

## TECHNOLOGY AND LINKED CHANGES

A logical counterpart to the preceding principle regarding the sequence of change is that *change breeds change.* That is, a change in one part of the system commonly produces related changes in other parts. Even a single technological innovation may set off a reaction which results in a series of linked changes. Again, White's scheme of cultural evolution whereby ideological changes followed sociological changes which were triggered by technological advance is one example as is the work of Murphy and Steward with tappers and trappers. In the latter case, both groups experienced changes in family structure, settlement patterns, and sociopolitical relations as a result of changes in economic structure. A particularly dramatic example of linked changes is offered by Lauriston Sharp in his documentation of the many changes which occurred among a group of Australian aborigines following the introduction of the steel axe.[16]

Following their initial recorded contact with a Dutch expedition in 1623 the Yir Yiront experienced only sporadic contacts with Europeans through the early part of the twentieth century. These were lethal for the Yir Yiront, however, as the whites killed them at will and kidnapped their children to use as slaves on their ranches. Finally their territory was set aside as a reserve and they were allowed to continue their traditional, stone-age way of life into the middle part of the twentieth century. In 1915 an Anglican mission began filtering a number of technological items to the group including the steel axe which rapidly replaced the aboriginal stone axe. The introduction of this particular tech-

nological innovation produced far-reaching effects which, in the end, led to the total disintegration of Yir Yiront culture and to the virtual demise of the people themselves. To understand how and why this happened it is necessary to look into the function and meaning of the stone axe which the steel axe replaced.

Only men could make and own the axe. Since stone for the heads was not available in their oceanside environment, they relied on an elaborate system of trading with their neighbors 400 miles to the south to obtain them. Every Yir Yiront male had at least one permanent trading partner with whom he exchanged spears tipped with sting ray spines for stone axe heads. The exchanges took place during large aboriginal congregations attended by hundreds and accompanied by all-important initiation rites and totemic ceremonials.

Within Yir Yiront society the axe was used by men, women, and children in any number of essential tasks including food and firewood gathering, building, and making tools and weapons. But since men retained ownership of the axe, women and children were required to borrow them. This borrowing proceeded through regular patterns of kinship behavior—axes were borrowed from husband, elder brother, or father but seldom from other kinfolk—and served to define and maintain a deeply ingrained system of status, sex, and role inequality. Women and children were dependent upon and subordinate to men, younger men were subordinate to older men, and younger brother was subordinate to elder brother. The borrowing of the stone axe, therefore, symbolized a theme of male superiority

16. Lauriston R. Sharp, "Steel Axes for Stone-Age Australians," in *Human Problems in Technological Change* Edward H. Spicer, ed. (New York: Russell Sage Foundation, 1952).

and dominance which permeated all important aspects of Yir Yiront culture and society.

The steel axe was introduced indiscriminately by trading stations and missions and was readily adopted because of its superior efficiency and longevity. This led to (1) confusion of sex, age, and kinship roles since younger men along with women and children could now own axes thereby negating the necessity of going through appropriate channels to borrow them, (2) weakening of traditional trading partnerships and consequent decline of aboriginal ceremonies where the exchanges had once taken place, and (3) loss of clearly defined leadership patterns. In the latter case, Sharp notes that initially leadership roles in working parties were assigned at the mission stations irrespective of age and kinship roles but that once away from the station, all men older than the leader would sleep while only those subordinate to him would work.

The introduction of the steel axe also affected Yir Yiront belief systems. Every element in their culture was accompanied by a myth which explained its existence, gave it meaning, and assigned it to a particular kinship group. Since no one was able to create a myth for the steel axe it could not be appropriately integrated into Yir Yiront culture—it did not "fit" existing patterns. Because of this, people became unsure of the other origin myths and confusion, doubt, and uncertainty set in. Sharp sums up the situation as follows:

The most disturbing effects of the steel axe, operating in conjunction with other elements also being introduced from the white man's several sub-cultures, developed in the realm of traditional ideas, sentiments and values. These were undermined at a rapidly mounting rate, without new conceptions being defined to replace them. The result was a mental and moral void which foreshadowed the collapse and destruction of all Yir Yiront culture, if not, indeed, the extinction of the biological group itself.[17]

## ECOLOGICAL ADAPTATION AND CHANGE

Another example of linked changes is provided by Ralph Linton's account of the change from dry to wet rice cultivation in Madagascar.[18] This also demonstrates how ecological factors—modifications in the physical environment—can set change in motion.

The Tanala are a hill tribe of western Madagascar who until about 250 years ago subsisted on the cultivation of dry rice using the slash and burn method. The land produced about two crops during a five year period and was then left for twenty-five years or so to regain its jungle growth and fertility. The Tanala would exploit all the land within easy reach of their villages and then move on to a new location to found another village. Given these conditions no concept of private property developed. The basic social organization consisted of large joint families headed by an adult male who shared residential proximity, cooperated in farming, and defended the group from hostile raiding parties. Produce was distributed evenly within the various households which made up the joint family. If one or more of these joint families suffered a bad crop they were given additional land in the proceeding year and since there was no market for any surplus, families planted only what they needed to sustain their numbers. Because of these factors, among others, no marked inequalities in wealth or status existed. The Tanala, then, were a classless society living in shifting, independent, and relatively isolated villages. The basic social unit was the joint family

17. Ibid., p. 85
18. Ralph Linton, *The Study of Man: An Introduction* (New York: Appleton-Century-Crofts, Inc., 1936).

working together on communal land and sharing the yield.

Wet rice cultivation, borrowed from the neighboring Betsileo, began as an adjunct to dry rice farming. From the start, wet rice terracing was conducted by single households since mobilization of the larger joint family was not required for such a small-scale enterprise. As wet rice cultivation caught on these single households kept using the same fields year after year because rotation was no longer necessary. This led to the development of the concept of private property. In addition, these households were reluctant to share their produce with the larger joint family which had no labor invested in it. Therefore, the formerly economically interdependent joint family system began breaking down and a class of landowners arose in a previously classless society. Those who did not acquire land in this way were forced to move further and further from the village in search of arable land and as these lands were far from the village center the people who farmed them began building their homes there. These new settlements became increasingly household rather than joint family ventures so that further fragmentation took place.

The joint family system suffered further disintegration where periodic village moving was concerned. Joint families had once moved together. Now though, those households with vested interests in wet rice terraces stayed behind while landless households moved on. This led to further disintegration of the joint family as new villages were now made up of households from different families. Each time a new village was formed some of these households would acquire permanent land rights and others would move on repeating the process again. Eventually, then, Tanala territory was spotted with settled villages in which the single household was the basic social unit.

Several factors combined to unite these independent villages into a tribal society. Old patterns of warfare between villages broke down because the now permanent villages were more easily fortified and were less vulnerable to attack. The joint families retained religious activities so that a lot of visiting took place between villages. This encouraged more intervillage marriages. In addition, slaves became a valuable commodity as workers on the rice terraces and further intervillage bonds were established in regularizing the relationships between slaves and their masters. The final transformation was accomplished around 1840 when one of the lineages established domination over several others, declared itself royal, and named its senior member king. Linton comments:

It was a far cry from the mobile, self-contained Tanala villages with their classless society and strong joint families to the Tanala Kingdom with its central authority, settled subjects, rudimentary social classes based on economic differences, and lineages of little more than ceremonial importance. However, the transformation can be traced step by step and at every step we find irrigated rice at the bottom of the change. It created a condition which necessitated either a modification of preexisting patterns or the adoption of patterns already developed in the neighboring tribes who had had a longer time to meet these problems.[19]

### SUMMARY

Diffusion exhibits many different characteristics. It is a selective process, proceeds at varying rates, is reciprocal, and goes in both directions. It is effected by the duration and intensity of contact, similarity of the two groups, and relative cultural integration. New items are commonly sub-

19. Ibid., p. 353.

jected to reinterpretation in form, function, or meaning by the receiving group and some areas of culture are more resistant to change than others although considerable debate surrounds this issue. The example of the introduction of the steel axe to the Yir Yiront shows how a technological change can set off a series of linked changes while the Tanala example demonstrates that similar results can occur with a change in ecological adaptation. Some of these characteristics are further reflected in the consideration of acculturation which follows.

### For Further Reading

Coleman, J. S.; E. Katz; and H. Menzel *Medical Innovation: A Diffusion Study.* Indianapolis, Indiana: Bobbs-Merrill Book Company, 1966. A systematic study of the adoption of a new drug by doctors in the Midwest. In tracing the adoption process the authors discover that social networks among the practicing physicians are of particular importance.

Erasmus, C. J. *Man Takes Control: Cultural Development and American Aid.* New York: The Bobbs-Merrill Book Company, 1961. Erasmus covers change processes in the first part of this book and then offers a lengthy description and analysis of a successful change program in northern Mexico.

Foster, G. M. *Traditional Cultures and the Impact of Technological Change.* 2nd ed. New York: Harper & Row Publishers, 1973. A revised edition of an earlier work of the same name. Foster discusses the general processes of change with particular emphasis on psychological, social, and cultural barriers and stimulants to change.

Goodenough, W. *Cooperation and Change: An Anthropological Approach to Community Development.* New York: The Russell Sage Foundation, 1963. The better part of this volume is devoted to an analysis of culture and change while the latter part

focuses on practical problems in community development. Students should find the chapter on "The Dimensions of Community Change" particularly helpful.

Herskovitz, M. J. *Cultural Dynamics.* New York: Alfred A. Knopf, 1947. Abridged from a larger work, this book presents a concise review of the change literature through the early 1940s and the author offers his own notions about change derived from the "American Historical School."

Rogers, E. M. with F. F. Shoemaker *Communication of Innovations: A Cross-Cultural Approach.* New York: The Free Press, 1971. An expanded version of an earlier book called *The Diffusion of Innovations,* this work undertakes an extensive review of the literature on diffusion with evaluations and conclusions regarding successful and unsuccessful innovation efforts. A useful appendix presents many of the generalizations which have been made about diffusion and lists the works which do or do not support each generalization. It is a good start on a more unified theory of change and is highly recommended.

### Bibliography

Bruner, E. M. 1956. "Cultural Transmission and Culture Change," *Southwestern Journal of Anthropology* 12: 191-199.

Foster, G. M. 1960. *Culture and Conquest: America's Spanish Heritage.* Viking Fund Publications in Anthropology 27. Chicago: Quadrangle Books, Inc.

Gluckman, M. 1940. "Analysis of a Social Situation in Modern Zululand." *Bantu Studies* 14: 91-146.

Hagen, E. E. 1962. *On the Theory of Social Change: How Economic Growth Begins* Homewood, Ill.: The Dorsey Press.

Hoebel, E. A. 1972. *Anthropology: The Study of Man* 4th ed. New York: McGraw Hill Book Company.

Holmes, L. D. 1965. *Anthropology: An Intro-*

duction. New York: The Ronald Press Company.

Keesing, F. M. 1952. *Culture Change: An Analysis and Bibliography of Anthropological Sources to 1952.* Stanford: Stanford University Press.

Lindgren, E. J. 1938. "An Example of Culture Contact Without Conflict: The Reindeer Tungus and the Cossacks in Northwestern Manchuria," *American Anthropologist* 40: 605-662.

Linton, R. 1936. *The Study of Man: An Introduction.* New York: Appleton-Century-Crofts, Inc.

Mandelbaum, D. G. 1941. "Culture Change Among the Nilgiri Tribes," *American Anthropologist* 43: 19-26.

Mead, M. 1928. *Coming of Age in Samoa.* New York: William Morrow and Company.

———. 1956. *New Lives for Old: Cultural Transformation–Manus, 1928-1953.* New York: William Morrow and Company.

Moore, W. E. 1963. *Social Change.* New York: Prentice-Hall.

Rogers, E. M. with Shoemaker, F. F. 1971. *Communication of Innovations: A Cross-Cultural Approach.* New York: The Free Press.

Sharp, R. L. 1952. "Steel Axes for Stone-Age Australians." In *Human Problems in Technological Change,* ed. E. H. Spicer. New York: The Russell Sage Foundation.

Turnbull, C. 1962. *The Forest People.* New York: Doubleday Book Company.

Vogt, E. Z. 1960. "On the Concepts of Structure and Process in Cultural Anthropology," *American Anthropologist* 62: 18-33.

Weber, M. 1953. *The Protestant Ethic and the Spirit of Capitalism.* New York: Charles Scribner and Sons.

# 4 | Acculturation

Acculturation is a special kind of diffusion which occurs when two previously autonomous cultural traditions come into continuous contact with sufficient intensity to promote extensive changes in one or both. This kind of change is qualitatively different from the diffusion of single traits and complexes in that it may involve the total reorganization of one or both groups in a relatively short period of time. Although anthropologists have tended to focus on drastic change in a subordinate group under the influence of a dominant group with which it has come into contact, the situation and the results can vary greatly. Stable readjustment may be achieved, one group may become extinct, assimilation may occur, or one may be incorporated into the other as a subculture. Of course, as we have seen above, contact itself is not always sufficient to lead to such changes.

The best documented, and perhaps most dramatic, example of acculturation on record is that which occurred with the intrusion of the Spaniards into Mexico. Prior to the Spanish conquest in the early part of the sixteenth century, the Aztec upper class dominated central and southern Mexico. A number of native groups were dissatisfied with this domination and sided with the Spanish in the conquest. Thus the Tlaxcalans from Mexico's south

Atlantic seaboard and inland were instrumental in the fall of Tenochtitlán, the Aztec capital and seat of power.[1] With the fall of the Aztecs, many peoples formerly dominated by them peacefully accepted Spanish control. So it was that about 2,500 Spaniards were able to conquer and subsequently control a nation whose numbers at the time of conquest have been estimated as high as ten million.[2] This has been further explained as follows:

In the first place, the Spaniards simply moved into the position in the existing social structure that had previously been occupied by the Aztec upper class. Native rulers friendly to the new regime were allowed to keep their positions; many became rapidly and thoroughly hispanicized. Intermarriage was frequent. The native religion had been closely bound up with the power of the dominant Aztec group, and when it was defeated, it lost much prestige. Christianity thus found easy acceptance among peoples who were already hospitable toward new religious ideas. For large segments of the population the Spanish conquest made little change in

---

1. For an interesting account of this Indian-Spanish cooperation, see, Charles Gibson, *Tlaxcala in the Sixteenth Century*, 2nd ed. (Stanford: Stanford University Press, 1967).
2. Ralph Beals and Harry Hoijer, *An Introduction to Anthropology*, 4th ed. (New York: Macmillan, 1971), p. 603.

political participation or economic life; they continued to cultivate their ancestral lands in much the same fashion as before and paid the same tribute to the government, now Spanish rather than Indian.[3]

Where later control was concerned it should be added that the Spanish church and state cooperated in brutal exploitation of the population. Appropriation of Indian lands, forced labor, and movement of whole populations to work in the mines and ranches to the north was common. These tactics, along with destruction of what lands the Indians were left with through the results of cattle grazing, use of the plow, and Spanish acquisition of needed water supplies—and the introduction of European diseases—led to a two-thirds decline in the native population by 1650.[4]

In spite of these early hardships the Indians eagerly accepted European culture. New generations grew out of the intermarriage of Indian and Spanish and the hispanization of whole native populations took place. These people lived in Spanish dominated towns, spoke the Spanish language, and adopted Spanish lifeways. By 1950, 90 percent of Mexico's population had followed this pattern. The other 10 percent (2.5 million)[5] of Mexico's population retain their Indian identity but they too have lost the basic patterns of the aboriginal culture. This serves to illustrate the basic nature of the acculturative process. Ralph Beals and Harry Hoijer in their popular introductory anthropology text reflect on this point:

...the Indian cultures...are mainly the result not of retention and development of pre-conquest elements, but rather of the retention and readaptation of sixteenth- and seventeenth-century Spanish cultural traits...these elements, modified and reworked, have been so integrated with aboriginal cultural patterns as to result in completely new cultural wholes,

which are amalgams, not simple mixtures, of Spanish and Indian traits...new creations that have emerged from a fusion of both the Spanish and the Indian traditions.[6]

Acculturation, like all sociocultural change, is an individual phenomenon although it can be conceptualized at either the group or individual level. We can draw examples of both approaches from research conducted in the highlands of Guatemala. Just south of Mexico, the Republic of Guatemala has a total population slightly over five million.[7] About half of these people are Mayan Indians who reside primarily in the highland regions. Two-thirds of the Indian population inhabit the western highlands adjacent to Mexico which makes this region the largest remaining heartland of Indian culture and society in the Americas.[8] In the midwestern highlands the towns surrounding Lake Atitlán provide a good example of the surviving Mayan cultural patterns. A combination of historical, geographical, and cultural factors have produced considerable variability from one town to the next although they all share a broad pattern of cultural similarity. Since we will return to a discussion of this region in considering community development and modernization, some detail concerning the similarities and differences in cul-

3. Ibid.
4. Eric R. Wolf, *Sons of the Shaking Earth* (Chicago: University of Chicago Press, 1959).
5. Anselmo Marino Flores, "Indian Population and its Identification," in *Handbook of Middle American Indians*, Manning Nash, ed., vol. 6 University of Texas Press, 1967), pp. 12-25.
6. Beals and Hoijer, *An Introduction to Anthropology*, p. 605.
7. Dirección General de Estadística, *VIII Censo de Poblacion y III de Habitacion* (Guatemala, C. A., 1973).
8. Manning Nash, "Guatemalan Highlands," in *Handbook of Middle American Indians*, Evon Vogt, ed., vol. 7 (Austin: University of Texas Press, 1969), pp. 30-45.

tural and social patterning will be outlined here.

The community is the locus of ethnic and social identity, each manifesting a relatively distinct costume, dialect, mythology, economic specialization, and round of socioreligious arrangements. Ecological variation along with endogamously tied skills and economic pursuits promotes a mutual interdependence which is expressed in a system of rotating local, regional, and national markets.[9] The peasant economy—small plot subsistence agriculture utilizing a simple technology to produce the preconquest trinity of maize, beans, and squash—has been accurately described as " . . .a money economy organized in single households as both consumption and production units, with a strongly developed market which tends to be perfectly competitive."[10]

While change in this region has been continuous since the conquest—the acculturation process here was basically the same as that described for Mexico—a series of events in the last eighty years have produced a more dynamic environment of change. Coffee became a major export crop in Guatemala around the turn of the century. This encouraged the intrusion of non-Indian Guatemalans (Ladinos) and foreigners into the highlands to exploit the new wealth potential of Indian labor and land. These outsiders brought their own cultural traditions, schools, technology, roads, and the notion of racial and cultural superiority—which subordinated the Indian and his way of life. National political changes transformed native political institutions, replacing local control by village elders with Ladino-dominated local and regional political structures. Seasonal labor migration, commercial activities, military service, and mass communication have brought the Indian societies into closer contact with the outside world. More recently, ac-

tive religious proselytizing, an influx of tourists, and a number of variously conceived aid programs have provided further impetus to the change process.

The impact of these events, however, has been far from uniform. In fact, differential exposure to change influences along with variable community reaction to these has served to perpetuate, and in some cases greatly increase, the sociocultural diversity extant from one local society to the next. In some communities men wear Western style dress, converse in Spanish, work in nonagricultural pursuits, go to doctors when someone in their families becomes ill, and take little part in religious activities. In others, they retain the distinctive Indian costume, speak little or no Spanish, rely on subsistence agriculture for their livelihood, go to native practitioners in time of illness, retain use of the sweat bath for curing and bathing, and maintain the social and religious life of their communities through rotating service in a series of ranked civil and religious offices—the civil-religious hierarchy.

In discussing these changes in Guatemalan Indian communities Richard Adams has distinguished between individual and group acculturation, or "ladinoization" as the acculturation process is commonly tagged in Guatemala.[11] Individual ladinoization involves social mobility whereby new habits are learned and the person moves into a new social category—that of the Ladino. To this day the process

9. Manning Nash, "Indian Economies," in *Handbook of Middle American Indians*, Manning Nash, ed., pp.87-102.

10. Sol Tax, *Penny Capitalism: A Guatemalan Indian Economy* Smithsonian Institute, Institute of Social Anthropology Publication no. 16 (Washington, D.C., 1953), p. 13.

11. Richard N. Adams, *Cultural Surveys of Panama-Guatemala-El Salvador-Honduras* Pan American Sanitary Bureau, Scientific Publication no. 33 (Washington, D.C., 1957).

of individual mobility in the highland regions requires that, in addition to acquiring Ladino lifeways, the individual must move to a town where his ethnic identity is not know in order to "pass" into the Ladino stratum of society. So it is that those who live as Ladinos in other areas are regarded socially and culturally as Indians—and so treated—when they return to their native villages to visit friends and relatives. We will return to this process of individual change following a discussion of group acculturation.

## GROUP ACCULTURATION

Group change, according to Adams, differs from individual change in that social mobility is not involved and the individual is one of an entire segment of society involved in establishing new norms and altering the internal customs of the group. The whole community gradually sheds Indian customs, becoming more Ladino-like and less Indian-like. Several transitional types, or stages, are proposed as acculturation progresses. Moving from most to least Indian these ideal types are (1) the traditional Indian community, (2) the modified Indian community, and (3) the Ladinoized Indian community. At the final point of the continuum all Indian traits have been lost and the group passes into the Ladino category.[12] The traditional Indian community has

...retained to some degree a distinct socio-political-religious organization, both men and women have some distinctive features of clothing, most of the women and some of the men are still monolingual (speaking only an Indian language), and the use of Indian surnames is still very common...[other traits may include]...use of the temescal (sweat bath), the retention, although perhaps in an attenuated form, of the Maya calendar, the use of a highly developed system of diviners and curers, etc.

As we move towards the *modified Indian community* a number of Indian traits become weakened or lost, and there is a crystallization of Indianism around another group of traits. Those lost or weakened include:

...the political religious organization and the distinctive dress of the men...all the men and many of the women become bilingual, but the Indian language is still retained as the mother tongue...women generally retain distinctive clothing, although it may not always be possible to identify one's village by the nature of the costume...the use of the temescal often disappears, the Maya calendar is usually no longer functional, and the curers and diviners find considerable competition from Ladino spiritualists and other lay curers.

The modified Indians, however, retain many traits which set them aside as clearly Indian such as:

...the women's distinctive costume, the leadership of the men in religious activities...cooking still done between three stones on the floor...the men still use the tumpline for carrying goods, and the community retains its integrity as an Indian community. The people still manifest resistance to one of their members becoming a Ladino through the adoption of Ladino customs.[13]

In *Ladinoized Indian communities* most observable Indian traits have disappeared. Neither sex retains distinctive dress, speaks an Indian language, or carries an Indian surname. The shoulder and pack animals have replaced the tumpline for carrying loads. On the other hand, distinguished from Ladinos, the men still lead in religious rituals, cooking on the floor is preferred, and the group is still territorially distinct. Ladinos still see them as sub-

12. Ibid.
13. Adams, *Cultural Surveys of Panama-Guatemala-El Salvador-Honduras,* pp. 271-72.

ordinate and Indian although they share the poverty and much of the life-style of the lower-class Ladinos. In effect they have lost most of the Indian sociocultural patterns but have yet to enter fully into the Ladino class.

This example of acculturation in Guatemalan Indian communities shows important differences *between* groups (intercultural diversity) and provides a useful scheme for categorizing different communities on gross indices of change as they move from Indian to Ladino. As Adams is well aware, however, it glosses over the important differences *within* communities (intracultural diversity) as individuals react in different ways and at different rates to the impetus of change. We can draw an example of this latter kind of change from research conducted by the writer in one of these highland communities.[14]

**INDIVIDUAL ACCULTURATION**

San Lucas Tolimán fits handily into Adams' scheme as a modified Indian community. It is one of the towns previously mentioned as being situated on the shores of Lake Atitlán in the midwestern highlands. The population consists of 3,214 Indians (81 percent) and 761 Ladinos (19 percent). While this biethnic distinction implies one population of Spanish-European ancestry and another whose forebears in the New World predate the Spanish conquest, considerable interbreeding has taken place and the contemporary distinction is based less on biological than sociocultural factors. What we actually see are groups which are distinguished by distinct sociocultural patterns with some racial and historical parallels.

Generally speaking, Ladinos speak Spanish, wear Western style dress, practice nominal Catholicism, tend towards nonagricultural occupations, are better edu-

cated, economically better disposed, and manifest superior housing, sanitation, diet, and health than do the Indians. The Indian sociocultural pattern, as presented above, differs significantly. In addition, both groups tend to see the Ladino and his way of life as superior to that of the Indian.

Of the many changes taking place within the native San Lucas population, dress and language are perhaps the most obvious. Only a small minority of the males wear the distinctive Indian costume which was once a symbol of community identification. The women have adopted the generalized factory-made costume worn in many of the communities throughout the highlands, so they cannot be identified by the native San Lucas dress either. Cakchiquel, the native dialect of Maya-Quiche, remains the primary language for the population although most of the males and a majority of the females exhibit varying degrees of facility with Spanish. Changes in family organization and residential patterns are also evident. Where in the past several related families shared a similar residence plot and cooperated in socioreligious activities, the tendency now is towards nuclear families living on separate plots of land.

Changes in household construction and services are less apparent although some Indians have given up their *ranchos* (straw roof, mud and cane walls, dirt floor) for Ladino style *casas* (tin roof, hard walls, covered floors) and a small number have adopted the raised cooking hearth. While the majority of Ladino homes have sanitary facilities, running water, electricity, a

14. For basic descriptive information on this community, see, Clyde M. Woods, *Medicine and Culture Change in San Lucas Toliman: A Highland Guatemalan Community,* Ph.D. dis (Stanford University, 1968) and idem, "San Lucas Toliman," in *Los Pueblos del Lago Atitlán* Sol Tax, ed. (Guatemala: Seminario de Integracion Social, 1968).

## FIGURE C

### CHANGES IN TRADITIONAL INDIAN PRACTISES IN SAN LUCAS TOLIMÁN[15]

| Trait | Indian | | Ladino | |
|---|---|---|---|---|
| | With | Without | With | Without |
| Spanish Language (males) | 89% | 11% | 100% | 00% |
| Modern Dress (males) | 84 | 16 | 100 | 00 |
| No Sweat Bath | 84 | 16 | 100 | 00 |
| Nuclear Household | 71 | 29 | 77 | 23 |
| Single Residence Plot | 63 | 37 | 94 | 06 |
| Residence Plot Ownership | 40 | 60 | 75 | 25 |
| School Population in School | 22 | 78 | 97 | 03 |
| Sanctioned Marital Union | 21 | 79 | 77 | 23 |
| Sanitary Facilities | 17 | 83 | 86 | 14 |
| Non-Agricultural Occupation | 14 | 86 | 73 | 27 |
| Shoes | 13 | 87 | 91 | 09 |
| Radio | 09 | 91 | 57 | 43 |
| Ladino Style House | 08 | 92 | 94 | 06 |
| Raised Cooking Hearth | 04 | 96 | 96 | 04 |
| Running Water | 03 | 97 | 58 | 42 |
| Electricity | 02 | 98 | 44 | 56 |
| Domestic Help | 01 | 99 | 43 | 57 |

radio, and employ domestic help, only a handful of Indian households boast such luxuries. A particularly significant departure from tradition is the diminishing use of the sweat bath which played a central role in curing practices, bathing, and postnatal care of mother and child. Only a minority of families retain these practices.

A number of other changes can be summarily noted. Courting is more open than in the past and marriage by elopement offers an alternative to the traditional marriage-by-contract between the two sets of parents. This has been accompanied by an increase in legally consummated unions. There has been some increase in school attendance although there is still little value placed on education. This reflects economic realities: along with limited opportunities for nonagricultural employment, time spent in school is time lost in the home (girls) and in the fields (boys). The overwhelming majority of the Indians remain subsistence farmers and heavy loads are still carried with the tumpline. Where curing practices are concerned traditional curers are meeting stiff competition from Ladino lay curers, spiritualists, and Western-trained medical doctors and nurses. A summary of these changes in the Indian way of life in San Lucas are outlined in Figure C.

Perhaps the most significant departures from tradition in San Lucas can be seen in the decline of the civil-religious hierarchy. The social, political, and religious life in Guatemalan Indian communities has been

15. Adapted from Clyde M. Woods and Theodore D. Graves, *The Process of Medical Change in a Highland Guatemalan Town* (Los Angeles: Latin American Center, University of California, 1973), p. 9.

traditionally maintained by brotherhoods whose members share civil and ceremonial responsibility through alternating service in a series of interrelated and ranked offices. This all-important Indian institution has remained intact in some of the lake communities but its importance has diminished considerably in others. The reasons for this are multiple but, as in San Lucas, they generally involve varying degrees of alienation from traditional Indian patterns by members of the population. Many, particularly those who are younger, have served in the military, and have been more exposed to the outside world, choose to invest their time and money in an effort to improve their own economic position rather than serving costly one-year periods of community service every three or four years. In addition, various subsidiary service and religious groups compete for Indian loyalty and once recruited by these rival groups they no longer serve in the traditional offices.

In San Lucas the system is clearly waning. Its political functions have been almost totally usurped by the local, regional, and national Ladino power structure and its role in the socioreligious life of the community is being effectively threatened by competing organizations. While 81 percent of the Indians are Catholic, many of these have switched to reformed Catholicism as interpreted by newly resident priests and nonlocal catequists and no longer serve in the religious offices. Another 13 percent of the population have converted to one of the three Protestant sects in San Lucas (6 percent of the Indians claim no religious affiliation whatsoever) and the fundamentalist doctrines of these groups forbid participation in the religious offices, since they are against the smoking, drinking, and dancing which commonly accompany traditional rituals. The semi-pagan rituals themselves, of course, are the clinchers and are held in similar disdain

by reformed Catholics and much of the resident Ladino population. These factors, among others, have combined to reduce the number of men available for service in the ceremonial offices. This increases the burden of responsibility and requires more frequent periods of service for those still willing to serve, thereby further weakening the system and making eventual dissolution more probable. Below, we will consider in more detail the breakdown of the civil-religious hierarchy in another lake town.

Consequent with these changes is a less obvious but significant shift in traditional world view. Sol Tax and other students of Guatemalan Indian communities have noted the homogeneity and tenacity of traditional systems of belief in the face of apparent changes in material culture.[16] This appeared not to be the case in San Lucas so a questionnaire containing forty-eight traditional beliefs was designed and orally administered to a sample of forty Indian males to test the degree of homogeneity and tenacity of the belief system there.[17] Each respondent was asked if he

16. For example, see, Sol Tax and Robert Hinshaw, "Panajachel a Generation Later," in *The Social Anthropology of Latin America*, Walter Goldschmidt and Harry Hoijer, eds. (Essays in honor of Ralph Beals) (Los Angeles: Latin American Center, University of California, 1970); Ruben Reina, *Chinautla: A Guatemalan Indian Community*, Middle American Research Institute, Tulane University, Publication no. 24 (1960); and Manning Nash, *Machine Age Maya* (Chicago: University of Chicago Press, 1958).

17. Most of these beliefs were taken from a list originally collected by Sol Tax in 1936 and subsequently supplemented by Robert Hinshaw in 1964. These were pretested in San Lucas and forty-eight selected which were common in the community. They include such beliefs as a pregnant woman who ventures out in an eclipse will have a deformed child; misfortune is more likely to occur on certain bad days and hours; special people can turn into animals at night and do evil things to others; children who play at crossroads will become sick because evil spirits cross there; fighting cats in the patio at night signify impending misfortune; and so on.

was aware of each belief and whether he accepted or rejected its validity. The scores range from a low of eleven to a high of forty-six beliefs accepted as valid with an average score of twenty-eight. These findings clearly suggest that belief is neither homogeneous or rigidly tenacious in San Lucas. Significantly, many respondents were aware of beliefs which they no longer regarded as valid. Commensurate with our other findings, then, considerable intracommunity variability is manifested in belief as well as behavior. The Indians in San Lucas are beginning to shed their traditional view of the world.

In spite of these observed variations on traditional patterns in San Lucas it would be a mistake to disregard the fact that it is still an Indian community. The Indians are still set apart from their Ladino neighbors by a body of custom and belief, albeit in attenuated form, and by their own identification with the Indian community. Informants note that be it for economic opportunity, marriage, or other reasons it is still a drastic step for an Indian to sever ties with his own town. Marriage within the community is still the rule, those who put on Ladino airs are severely criticized, and marriage to local Ladinos remains a rare occurrence. In 1966 there were only fifteen mixed Ladino-Indian marriages in the community and all but 6 percent of the resident Indians were born there.

In sum, although the Indian population in San Lucas retains its integrity as an Indian community traditional patterns of behavior and belief are changing. The direction of change, as indicated by individual modifications in these patterns, is clearly toward the more modern Ladino way of life. Mutually reinforcing external and internal forces operate in this process: the quest for material goods and alternative life-styles leads to increasing involvement in the outside world and alienation from traditional social, political, and re-ligious institutions. As these institutions fail to meet the needs of a significant portion of the society and as cultural disorganization proceeds, the search for workable alternatives takes on an element of necessity. Thus, we find in this, and many like situations, an internal predisposition for external influence. In addition to the modernizing world around them, a particularly important influence is the relatively large resident Ladino population which offers an ever-present acculturative model.

These examples from Guatemala show that acculturation can be conceptualized at two levels. By comparing gross indices of change between groups we can portray whole communities at different stages on a continuum of acculturation. But this continuum is also manifested within communities as individuals in the group adopt innovations at different rates and times. This is true for both behavior and belief. Later we will return to this situation to consider the actual sequence of change, that is, which changes occur first.

## PSYCHOLOGICAL CONCOMITANTS OF ACCULTURATION

Anthropologists have also looked into the psychological consequences of acculturation. Since change often involves disintegration at the group level, it is not suprising that change can also lead to disruptive effects for the individual. A pioneering effort directed towards investigating these effects has been conducted by George and Louise Spindler among the Menomini Indians of Wisconsin in the early 1950s.[18] The Menomini sample was divided into five groups on the basis

18. George D. Spindler, *Sociocultural and Psychological Processes in Menomini Acculturation*, University of California Publications in Culture and Society, vol. 5 (1955).

of religious affiliation and other social characteristics such as income, group affiliation, and use of the native language to form a continuum from least to most acculturated. These groups are: (1) *Native Oriented*—the most traditional segment of Menomini as indicated by membership in the Medicine Lodge-Dream Dance groups; (2) *Peyote Cult*—a unique transitional group in that they share loss of identity and conflict because of acculturation with other transitional Menomini but retain a clear-cut identification as members of the cult; (3) *Transitional*—a larger transitional group exposed to a number of change influences including Western religions and lifeways but who are characterized by lack of significant participation in old or new religions: (4) *Lower-Status Acculturated*— those who have lost identification with traditional Indian patterns, are associated with the Catholic church, but have acculturated only to a laboring-class standard; and (5) *Elite Acculturated*—the most acculturated group who participate actively in the Catholic church, identify with Western lifeways, and hold more favorable socioeconomic positions.

A standard projective technique, the Rorschach or "inkblot" test, is then used to construct a "psychogram" for each of the groups. The Native Oriented group lack overt emotional responsiveness according to their "psychogram." They are inward oriented, fatalistic, exhibit quiet endurance under stress, and show no marked evidence of anxiety or internal conflict. Members of the Peyote Cult deviate in extreme form from all other groups in their preoccupation with rumination of the self, sin, salvation, and attainment of personal power through the ritual of Peyotism. The relaxing of emotions and overt expression of feelings experienced in these rituals allows them a unique adaptation in the transitional process. The other transitionals show the greatest signs of personality

disorganization and conflict produced by the acculturation situation.

Some are striving for an orderly way of life, toward goals recognizeable in the surrounding non-Indian community; others are withdrawn and mostly just vegetate; others go on destructive rampages, during or between drunks. Beatings, murders, illegitimacy, dirt, and disorder are a way of life . . .transitionals are like human populations everywhere who have lost their way; for them neither the goals of the traditional or the new culture are meaningful.[19]

The two acculturated Menomini groups deny their Indian identity and instead, identify with the culture of neighboring white groups. Psychologically they are emotionally open, achievement oriented, and react to pressure in a controlled but aggressive manner. In short, the acculturated Menomini, particularly the Elite, have learned how to stop being Menomini and be middle-class Americans. Further, this process occurs at both the sociological and psychological levels. In related research, the Spindlers found that Menomini women manifested less psychological change and disorganization than did the men. This is explained by the fact that in their traditional roles as wife and mother they come into less contact with disruptive acculturative influences and less is demanded of them.[20]

### REACTIVE MOVEMENTS

As we have seen from the preceeding examples, contact and the resulting changes, particularly when they emanate

19. George D. Spindler, "Psychocultural Adaptation," in *The Study of Personality* Edward Norbeck et al., eds. (New York: Holt, Rinehart, and Winston, 1968), p. 329.
20. Louise S. Spindler and George D. Spindler, "Male and Female Adaptations in Culture Change," *American Anthropologist*, 60 (1958):217-33.

from a dominant group, often cause disruptive and stressful effects on members of the receiving culture. Some groups experience reactionary movements as a response to these pressures in an attempt to restore meaning and content to their way of life. Anthropologists refer to these attempts as "Revitalization Movements" which are defined as deliberated, organized, conscious efforts by members of the society to construct a more satisfying and meaningful culture.[21] Although these movements share basic characteristics, they have been classified into subclasses as follows: (1) Nativistic Movements characterized by emphasis on the elimination of alien ideas, materials, and people; (2) Revivalistic Movements characterized by the reinstitution of lost or fading ideas and practices; (3) Cargo Cults characterized by the expected importation of alien ideas and goods which are part of a ship's cargo; (4) Vitalistic Movements characterized by the expectation of receiving alien elements but through other means than a ship's cargo; (5) Millenarian Movements characterized by an emphasis on the transformation of the world into an idealistic state through supernatural means; and (6) Messianic Movements characterized by a similar world transformation but through the medium of a divine saviour in human form.[22]

The Ghost Dance adopted by North American Indians during the nineteenth century in response to the white man's encroachment on Indian land and liberty provides a good example of a Nativistic Movement and also reveals elements of a Millenarian Movement. The basic theme involved the supernatural destruction of the white man and the restoration of the land to its unspoiled state prior to his coming. This theme, as we should expect, varied from tribe to tribe.

The Shoshone said a four day sleep would come over all believers, and they would awaken on

the fifth to a new world. Kiowa thought the new earth would slide from the west over the old one bearing buffalo and elk upon it...some Arapaho spoke of a wall of flame that would drive the whites back to their own country... The Walapai awaited a hurricane, the thunder of which would kill the whites and unbelievers.[23]

The adoption of various items of African culture by black Americans and the Black Muslim movement would be examples of Revivalistic Movements; A Vitalistic Movement might be exemplified by the selective borrowing of white cultural traits by the Indian Shakers; and Messianic Movements are illustrated by the growth of various religious traditions such as Christianity, Mohammedanism, and more recently, Bahai. Cargo Cults arose primarily in Melanesia in reaction to the pressures of contact with Western culture and are related to the importation of voluminous amounts of supplies by ship and plane during the two world wars—many of which were abandoned and left behind as forces retreated or moved on to further battles. One such movement, known as the Vailala Madness, took place in Papua after World War I.

This movement involved a kind of mass hysteria, in which numbers of natives were effected by giddiness and reeled about the village...The leaders of the movement poured forth utterances...which were in fact a mixture of nonsense syllables and pidgin English. Sometimes they were incomprehensible, but sometimes the leaders gave intelligible utterance to prophesies and injunction. The central theme of the former was that the ancestors

21. Anthony F. C. Wallace, "Revitalization Movements," *American Anthropologist*, 58 (1956):264-81.

22. Ibid., pp. 267-68.

23. Weston LaBarre, *The Ghost Dance: Origins of Religion* (Garden City, New York: Natural History Press, 1970), p. 230.

would soon return to the gulf in a ship, bringing with them a cargo of good things.[24]

These cults were intensified during the Second World War with the importation of a seemingly inexhaustible supply of goods and supplies and they continue into contemporary times. Natives in highland New Guinea have been photographed with miniature models of airplanes and runways presumably awaiting an aerial drop or landing and

In 1967, the most ambitious cult, which developed among the Sepik River Valley, proposed to dry up the river, after which a ribbon of concrete would unroll to form a superhighway up the river bed, along which fleets of trucks would flow, bringing cargo to the interior.[25]

### SUMMARY

The general process of acculturation was demonstrated by considering the Spanish conquest of Mexico and the resulting assimilation of the Spanish and Indian traditions. Examples from highland Guatemala showed that acculturation can be conceptualized at either the group or the individual level. Menomini Indian acculturation afforded a good example of the psychological consequences of changes of this type and our discussion of reactive movements demonstrated some of the ways in which the strains produced by change are manifested. Acculturation is often accompanied by programs of directed, or applied, change and this is the next topic to be covered.

### For Further Reading

Bohannon, P. and F. Plog, eds. *Beyond the Frontier*. Garden City, New York: The Natural History Press, 1967. An extensive selection of readings on change and acculturation from the many underdeveloped areas of the world. Minimal editorial comment.

Hogbin, I. *Social Change*. London: Watts, 1958. A well-written account of acculturation and change in Africa and Melanesia.

Linton, R., ed. *Acculturation in Seven American Indian Tribes*. New York: D. Appleton-Century-Crofts 1940. Good accounts of North American Indian acculturation by the anthropologists who studied them. Linton's concluding essay on acculturation is provocative but his attempts to tie the materials together in a general theoretical framework are not terribly successful.

Siegel, B. J., ed. *Acculturation: Critical Abstracts, North America*. Stanford: Stanford University Press, 1955. A summary of the theory, methods, and results of thirty-nine monographs and fifty-five journal articles dealing with North American Indian acculturation. Excellent reference manual.

Wallace, A.F.C. *Culture and Personality*. 2nd ed. New York: Random House, 1970. This book is recommended for several reasons. The chapter on "The Psychology of Cultural Change" is excellent, the problem of homogeneity versus diversity in anthropological research is discussed, and the theoretical framework for "revitalization movements" is presented.

Worseley, P. *The Trumpet Shall Sound: A Study of "Cargo" Cults in Melanesia*. London: Mac Gibbon and Kee, 1957. Reactive movements which took place in the South Pacific are described and placed in a comparative framework.

### Bibliography

Adams, R. N. 1958. *Cultural Surveys of Panama-Guatemala-El Salvador-Honduras*. Sci-

24. Ralph Piddington, *An Introduction to Social Anthropology*, vol. II (London: Oliver and Boyd, Ltd, 1957), p. 739.
25. E. Adamson Hoebel, *Anthropology: The Study of Man*, 4th ed. (New York: McGraw-Hill, 1972), pp. 666-67.

entific Publication 33 Washington: Pan American Sanitary Bureau.

Beals, R. L. and Hoijer, H. 1971. *An Introduction to Anthropology* 4th ed. New York: The Macmillan Company.

Dirección General de Estadística VIII Censo de Población y III de Habitación. 1973. Guatemala. C.A.

Gibson, C. 1967. *Tlaxcala in the Sixteenth Century*. 2d ed. Stanford: Stanford University Press.

Hoebel, E. A. 1972. *Anthropology: The Study of Man* 4th ed. New York: McGraw Hill Book Company.

LaBarre, W. 1970. *The Ghost Dance: Origins of Religion*. Garden City, New York: The Natural History Press.

Nash, M. 1958. *Machine Age Maya*. Chicago: University of Chicago Press.

———, ed. 1967. *Handbook of Middle American Indians* vol. 6. Austin: University of Texas Press.

Piddington, R. 1957. *An Introduction to Social Anthropology*. London: Oliver and Boyd, Ltd.

Reina, Ruben 1960. *Chinautla: A Guatemalan Indian Community*. New Orleans: Tulane University, Middle American Research Institute. Publication 24.

Spindler, G. D. 1955. *Sociocultural and Psychological Processes in Menomini Acculturation*. vol. 5. University of California Publications in Culture and Society.

———. 1968. "Psychological Adaptation." In *The Study of Personality*. ed. E. Norbeck. New York: Holt, Rinehart, and Winston.

Spindler, L. S. and Spindler, G. D. 1958. "Male and Female Adaptations in Culture Change," *American Anthropologist* 60: 217-233.

Tax, S. 1953. *Penny Capitalism: A Guatemalan Indian Economy*. Washington, D.C.: Smithsonian Institute, Institute of Social Anthropology, Publication 16.

Tax, S. and Hinshaw, R. 1970. "Panajachel a Generation Later." In *The Social Anthropology of Latin America Today*. ed. W. Goldschmidt and H. Hoijer. (Essays in Honor of Ralph Beals). Los Angeles: Latin American Center, University of California at Los Angeles, pp. 175-195.

Vogt, E. Z., ed. 1969. *Handbook of Middle American Indians,* vol. 7. Austin: University of Texas Press.

Wallace, A. F. C. 1956. "Revitalization Movements," *American Anthropologist* 58: 264-281.

Wolf, E. R. 1959. *Sons of the Shaking Earth*. Chicago: University of Chicago Press.

Woods, C. M. 1968. *Medicine and Culture Change in San Lucas Tolimán: A Highland Guatemalan Community*. Ph.D. diss. Stanford University.

———. 1968. "San Lucas Tolimán." In *Los Pueblos del Lago Atitlan* ed. Sol Tax Guatemala: Seminario de Integración Social.

Woods, C. M. and Graves, T. D. 1973. *The Process of Medical Change in a Highland Guatemalan Town*. Los Angeles: Latin American Center, University of California at Los Angeles.

# 5 | Directed Change

Directed change is the active and purposeful intervention of individuals or groups into the technological, sociological, and ideological practices of another people. In the conquest of Mexico outlined in chapter four, changes of this sort were imposed over three centuries. For example, the wooden-yoked, oxen-pulled plow was introduced to increase the efficiency of agriculture (but proved to be less efficient than aboriginal methods), the civil-religious hierarchy was offered as a more effective way of maintaining community civil and ceremonial functions, and Catholic missionaries energetically fought the evils of pagan beliefs in order to save the Indians from eternal damnation. In many parts of the world, missionaries, traders, explorers, and representatives of foreign governments and businesses have pursued various programs of directed change, suited primarily to their own needs. Much of the early research conducted by British anthropologists in their colonial territories was directed toward a better understanding of native institutions so that more effective colonial policies could be initiated.

## ANTHROPOLOGY AND DIRECTED CHANGE

For the most part, however, anthropologists, until quite recently, have been reluctant to take an active role in this area because of a principle, deeply ingrained in the discipline, that people have the sole right to choose their own destiny. This is closely related to the notion of "cultural relativity" which states that any practice is valid if considered within the cultural setting in which it takes place. By extension this implies that any given way of life is equally valid and cannot be judged by standards set in another culture. For this reason, the anthropologist's stance has been one of a detached observer—conducting his research without judging, condemning, or advocating change.

Many anthropologists today, however, have, by and large, accepted the fact that change is inevitable and that Western technology can aid in easing the poverty and misery apparent in many Third World countries. Because of this many have focused their research on the problems faced by peoples of the underdeveloped world as they make the transition to a more modern way of life. Still others have taken a more active role by serving as administrators and advisors of directed change programs. In addition, a number of books, manuals, and journals have been devoted to the topic of applied change.[1] Unfortunately,

1. See, for example, Edward H. Spicer, *Human Problems in Technological Change* (New York: The Russell Sage Foundation, 1952); Charles J. Erasmus,

change agents commonly ignore this literature and in so doing commit many costly and unnecessary errors. These are often due to such things as poor planning, failure to adequately communicate a clear understanding of the programs to the recipients, lack of foresight in gauging the effect of induced changes, and, perhaps most importantly, ignorance of local cultural patterns. A few examples should serve to illuminate these problems.

The introduction of the stove in village India produced some unexpected consequences. Cooking is traditionally done over an open, dung fire. There is no chimney and few windows so while the smoke slowly filters through the thatched roof, the smoke-filled room makes cooking unpleasant and contributes to respiratory and eye ailments. To combat this a cheap, chimneyed, fuel-saving stove was introduced. Its acceptance met with considerable objection, however, because the smoke had produced at least one desirable side effect: it kept out roof-destroying, wood-boring ants. So while the stove was inexpensive to purchase and operate, it was still more costly because roofs had to be constantly replaced.[2] In many other areas similar problems have been encountered because change agents have neglected to consider the role of an open fire as a source of heat and the role of smoke in keeping out pesky insects which often carry communicable diseases such as malaria (mosquito) and sleeping sickness (tsetse fly). The introduction of the stove, then, should be accompanied by a program of spraying and alternative forms of heat.

In San Lucas Tolimán, Guatemala a Catholic-sponsored cooperative introduced a model housing program. Inexpensive kerosene stoves replaced the traditional practice of cooking on the floor and small fireplaces were installed to compensate for the loss of heat. Unfortunately, the cost of kerosene for cooking and firewood for heating proved prohibitive. But ingenuity prevailed: The Indians simply placed their traditional open fire in the forward part of the fireplace.

In Afghanistan change agents encouraged the peasants to castrate their bulls at a young age so that they would grow larger and stronger. This innovation met with resistance and for good reason. Fields are tilled with a crude plow fastened to an equally crude yoke which is held in place by the large hump which develops on the shoulder of the mature animal. Bulls castrated at a young age do not develop this hump and therefore cannot be used in cultivating the fields.[3] The change agents might have introduced a new type of yoke along with castration such as the one widely used in Mexico which is lashed to the bull's head.

There have been many attempts to introduce hybrid corns to the many maize-producing regions of the world. These hybrids grow faster, are less susceptible to insect damage, contain more nutrients, and produce a higher yield. In many cases these innovations have failed because people prefer the color, texture, and taste of their old corn. In Bolivia one such program was successful—but not because the corn was preferred for making tortillas. It was very hard and consequently difficult to grind, but produced an excellent al-

Man Takes Control (New York: Bobbs-Merrill Company, 1961); George M. Foster, Traditional Cultures and the Impact of Technological Change, 2nd ed. (New York: Harper & Row, Publishers, 1973); Ward H. Goodenough, Cooperation in Change (New York: The Russell Sage Foundation, 1963); and Arthur H. Niehoff, A Casebook of Social Change (Chicago: Aldine Publishing Company, 1966). For an excellent treatment of problems and approaches involving medical change, see, Benjamin D. Paul, ed., Health, Culture, and Community (New York: The Russell Sage Foundation, 1955).

2. Foster, Traditional Cultures and the Impact of Technological Change, pp. 96-97.

3. Ibid., p. 97.

cohol to consume and sell. So the program resulted in increased drinking and alcoholism rather than an improved diet.[4]

Two further examples show how poor communication can lead to misunderstandings which seriously jeopardize directed-change efforts. A smallpox epidemic was taking many lives in Rhodesia so a team of doctors and nurses was sent to vaccinate the village populations. Their efforts were unsuccessful though since they found all the villages they entered were deserted. Finally they found a small boy and began interrogating him concerning the whereabouts of the population in one such village. Suddenly they were surrounded by spear-wielding natives who demanded that they release the boy. When one of the doctors angrily demanded an explanation for the natives' refusal to be vaccinated, the leader replied:

Six months ago our cattle were dying of something you called 'hoof and mouth disease' and you said 'we are your friends and have come to help you. Your cattle are dying and we can stamp out the disease.' We permitted you to help us and you killed all of our cattle.[5]

Finally, during World War II a navy officer gave a long lecture on the hazards of the common housefly to the population of a Pacific island village in an attempt to engage their cooperation in doing away with these pests. During the lecture he used a foot-long model of a fly for demonstrative purposes. He felt he had made his point until the chief remarked, "I can well understand your preoccupation with flies in America. We have flies here too, but they are just little fellows."[6]

These and many other kinds of problems which occur in change programs could be considerably alleviated if the recipients were subject to study prior to the introduction of innovations. Leaders could be located, lines of communication delineated, and factions which might come into conflict in a change situation found. Existing patterns of behavior and belief could be examined and the possible effects of change on these evaluated. More importantly, perhaps, the investigator could find out not only what the people need but what *they* themselves want, in the way of change. The anthropologist, with his interest in the whole way of life and the interconnections among the many parts of the sociocultural system, is particularly well-prepared to conduct such studies. Unfortunately, most of these kinds of studies to date have been done ex post facto—after the programs have been introduced. While these provide important theoretical and practical guidelines for change agents they remain a poor substitution for good prestudies in the actual communities where programs will be introduced.

One manual, based on information gleaned from the "after" studies mentioned above and prepared especially for agents of directed change, presents a model of the innovation process as shown in Figure D.

The line between the inception of the plan or idea to its integration within the social system is broken because successful integration is dependent upon the "action" and "reaction" of the innovator (change agent) and recipients (members of the receiving group), respectively. Seventeen different factors which commonly effect the integration of innovation(s) are also outlined and discussed in this manual. Three of these are regarded as particu-

4. Isabel Kelly, *La Antropologia, la Cultura y la Salud Publica* (Lima, Peru: Imprenta del SCISP, Ministry of Public Health and Social Welfare, 1960), pp. 10-11.

5. George M. Foster, *Traditional Cultures and the Impact of Technological Change* (New York, Harper & Row, Publishers, 1962), pp. 123-24.

6. Ibid., p. 122.

## FIGURE D

### MODEL OF THE INNOVATION PROCESS[7]

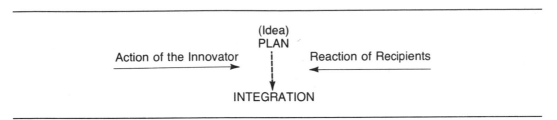

larly important where the "action" of the change agent is concerned: (1) the methods of communication used; (2) the kind of participation obtained from the recipients; and (3) the manner in which the innovation(s) is adapted to existing patterns. Where the "reaction" of the recipients is concerned, three additional factors are considered crucial: (1) whether they have an initial *felt need* for the innovation; (2) whether they perceive any practical benefit in its adoption; and (3) whether their traditional leaders are brought into the planning and implementation of the program. Where all or most of these factors are positive, an innovation has a favorable chance of acceptance.[8]

### THE INTRODUCTION OF MODERN MEDICINE IN HIGHLAND GUATEMALA

To evaluate the saliency of the factors mentioned above in the process of innovation we can consider the introduction of modern medicine in San Lucas Tolimán.[9] Endemic illness and the high death rate in San Lucas reflect inadequate nutrition, sanitation facilities, housing, and medical practices. All of this, of course, is related to extreme poverty—the average Indian wage (in 1966) is fifty cents a day, when work is available. The biggest killers are pulmonary and gastrointestinal diseases, and children, often suffering from malnutri-

tion, account for the overwhelming majority of deaths in any given period. San Lucas shares with the rest of Indian Guatemala one of the highest infant mortality rates in the world, and in 1965 over 61 percent of all deaths in the community were children who had not yet reached the age of five years. Given these and other considerations, it is not surprising that there is an obvious *felt need* for improved medical care in the community.

Although modern medicine has registered significant gains in San Lucas, there remains considerable reluctance on the part of the Indian population to relinquish the use of folk practitioners. This can be traced in part to shortcomings in modern medical programs introduced by a doctor who took residence in the community in 1963. An upwardly mobile, middle-class Ladino, he retained his most important social ties and a separate residence in Guatemala City. In San Lucas he aligned himself exclusively with the Ladino popu-

7. Adapted from Niehoff, *A Casebook of Social Change*, p. 11.

8. Ibid., pp. 40-41.

9. In addition to the references cited previously, see, Clyde M. Woods, "Medical Innovation in Highland Guatemala: The Case of San Lucas Toliman," in *Stranger In Our Midts: Guided Culture Change in Highland Guatemala*, P. Furst and K. Reed, eds. (Los Angeles: Latin American Center, University of California, 1970).

lation and was openly unsympathetic to the traditional Indian way of life. He was, admittedly, in the community to make money. His manner with patients was authoritarian and he was intolerant of those who did not demonstrate unqualified confidence in his abilities. These characteristics combined to produce a negative effect on his reputation in the community from the start.

When the doctor held a celebration to commemorate the first surgical operation performed in his clinic, the affair was attended by local and nonlocal Ladinos. No Indians were invited. During a grippe epidemic in 1966, he formed a committee to collect and distribute food and medicine to needy families. This was composed of the Ladino mayor, local Ladino businessmen, Ladino teachers, and several young Ladino girls on vacation from school in the nation's capital. When asked why no Indians were invited to participate the doctor replied, "The Indians are not interested and will not cooperate with us because they are busy with other things." Others on the committee expressed similar sentiments. It might be pointed out that about one-third of the Indians were "busy with other things"—they had the grippe! A similar antigrippe program conducted by the local parish did incorporate the aid of the Indian population. They openly cooperated and the program was no less successful than that of the doctor's.

Another barrier to the doctor's ready acceptance had to do with his "bedside manner." The native curer, or shaman, is bound by his calling to attend the sick even if the patient is unable to pay. This calling and the very essence of his office are deeply rooted in the basic assumptions of traditional Indian culture. The shaman becomes intimately involved in the curing process, both professionally and socially. Diagnosis and treatment are group affairs attended by family and friends and ac-

companied by ritual eating and drinking. His manner is friendly and unassuming, his diagnosis is relatively quick and is explained in terms the Indian can understand, and his treatment is unburdened by the use of complicated gadgetry and prolonged testing.

The doctor, on the other hand, performs his role as a means of livelihood. He does not share a set of common understandings with his Indian clients and has no culturally binding sanction to attend them. Patients must register with a teenage Ladino receptionist and then join the waiting throng. Patients are served on a first-come-first-served basis and occasionally must wait all day before being attended. Those who are unable to see the doctor in the day must pay from two to five dollars to see him after hours. The regular daytime fee is fifty cents plus the cost of medicine. The normal consultation is conducted without introductory pleasantries and on an impersonal, businesslike basis. Unless the patient is a child the examination is attended only by the patient and doctor, and perhaps a nurse. A few questions may be asked regarding symptoms, eating habits, and body functions but the doctor does not allude to any of the behavioral irregularities which the Indians believe lead to most illnesses. Any mention of a supernatural or behavioral cause is likely to be met with silence, or worse, ridicule. After the examination, the patient is turned over to a nurse who administers whatever treatment, instructions, medication, or prescriptions the case requires. Diagnosis, when offered at all, is couched in unfamiliar scientific terminology, and the patient leaves with little knowledge of his ailment or its cause.

Some of these alleged shortcomings of course are simply common characteristics of modern, Western medical practice. Among other things, however, the doctor could adapt his behavior to the particular situation, be more sympathetic to traditional and deeply ingrained patterns of belief and behavior, and enlist Indian cooperation in community projects. Another possible move to aid the Indians in making the transition from traditional to modern medicine might be to enlist the aid of members of the Indian community as helpers and interpreters in the clinic. Lay curers sympathetic to modern medicine could also be used, but one of the local pharmacists would be ideal. These practitioners constantly use modern medicinal preparations in their business and, in addition, are well versed in Indian explanations and feelings about illness.

In spite of these shortcomings, modern medicine is definitely making significant headway in San Lucas. Even though the doctor has failed to adapt his methods to existing patterns, incorporate Indian leadership, and communicate his message through appropriate channels, a large portion of the population is actively participating as patients—even though they may be using traditional curers at the same time. In fact, the patient load in 1966 was more than one doctor could handle. It would appear in this case that a strong *felt need* for improved medical care coupled with clear evidence of *practical benefit* is sufficient to outweigh the negative factors. In short, modern medicine works.

### PARTICIPANT INTERVENTION IN PERU

One directed change program, initiated by Cornell University's Alan Holmberg and various associates, involved a pre-study, the introduction of multiple innovations, and continuing observations of the changes which followed.[10] This program of *Participant Intervention*, conducted in Vicos, Peru, was twofold in purpose. Theoretically members of the project wanted to conduct experimental research on the process of change, and

practically they wanted to assist the community in making the transition from a position of dependence and submission in a highly provincial world to one of relative independence and freedom within the larger framework of national life.

Vicos is situated in a high valley in the Andes about 250 miles from the Peruvian capital of Lima. A population of 2,250 Quechua-speaking Indians live on scattered homesteads of from one to fifteen acres practicing subsistence agriculture with such crops as oca, corn, potatoes, wheat, and chile. They also practice limited animal husbandry. Like many other properties in the Andes, Vicos was a hacienda which belonged to the state and was leased at public auction to the highest bidder every ten years. The leasee, who paid $500 a year in this case, received about 10 percent of hacienda land for commercial cultivation along with free Indian labor and services. One adult member from each of 380 families was obligated to work three days each week for the leasee and, in addition, the Indians were required to supply animals for agricultural work and provide free services as shepherds, grooms, watchmen, cooks, and servants.

In 1952 the industrial firm renting Vicos went bankrupt and Cornell University in cooperation with the Peruvian Indian Institute picked up the last five years of the lease. A Peruvian anthropologist had already been working in Vicos for several years so considerable information on the community was already available. When

10. More detailed descriptions of this project can be found in Allan R. Holmberg, "Changing Community Attitudes and Values in Peru: A Case Study in Guided Change," *Social Change In Latin America Today*, Council on Foreign Relations (New York: Random House, Vintage Books, 1960) and Henry F. Dobyns, Paul L. Doughty, and Harold D. Laswell, eds., *Peasants, Power, and Applied Social Change: Vicos as a Model* (Beverly Hills: Sage Publications, 1964).

people from Cornell came on the scene the Indians had little political power and the society was poorly integrated. Relationships beyond the immediate family were characterized by lack of cooperation, suspicion, and hostility. Stealing, both from the hacienda and one's neighbors, was common. Holmberg comments that several hundred years of domination by the hacienda system had left the Indians in a subordinate, powerless, and economically depressed situation and produced attitudes of distrust, fear, and hate for the outside world. In addition, the land had lost most of its fertility, seeds had degenerated, crops and animals were stunted and diseased, 80 percent of the people were infected with parasites, illness was rampant, and infant mortality extremely high.

Given this situation the Cornell project group decided to focus their initial efforts on three major areas: (1) economics and technology; (2) education; and (3) nutrition and health. To even begin, however, they had to make changes in the social organization and establish community cooperation. The plan was to develop independent problem-solving and decision-making organizations within the indigenous community so that they could gradually assume control and direction of their own affairs. A group of elected leaders was organized and in consultation with them the project members drew up an integrated plan of community development. The basic mode of operation involved weekly meetings of the labor force where problems, programs, and progress were discussed. Results of these meetings were then turned over to special committees for consideration and their decisions were discussed again at the next weekly meeting. In addition, the project called for the use of Indian leaders as supervisory personnel on the hacienda rather than outsiders, the replacement of free services with salaried employees, and the investment of all hacienda profits back into the community development program. A few examples of community progress are worthy of note.

One divisive source of in-group strife was disagreement over ownership of cattle which were grazed together and carried no special distinguishing marks of ownership other than their outward appearance. Rustling was common and lots of time and money was wasted on disputes over ownership. It was decided that branding might solve the problem but this was initially rejected. In an open community meeting it was discovered that owners of small herds would not brand their cattle because they felt the large cattle owners would not brand theirs. Their rationale was that the owners of large herds would not risk showing them off in public because, given the size of their herds, many were probably acquired through rustling. Finally a powerful member of the community, who owned many cattle, brought them all in for branding thereby proving his innocence. Others followed, and a successful program ensued.

The potato crop, which is the basic staple in Vicos, was destroyed by blight causing extreme economic hardships. To insure that this would not reoccur the project supplied technical advise in the form of information on adequate preparation of the soil, use of healthy and disinfected seed, proper weeding, and periodic spraying with insecticides. While the Indians saw value in this plan many would not adopt it because they were still suspicious of outsiders, many could not afford the investment, and others had too little land. This resistance to innovation was solved by providing a small group of families with financial aid until their harvest came in. The pragmatic benefit of adopting the new practices was realized when these families doubled their harvest in the first year. By the end of Cornell University's lease the yield of the potato crop had increased 400 percent and it had become a commercial cash crop as well as a staple. Yields were similarly increased for a number of other agricultural products.

Education, both formal and informal, was a major goal of the project since the members felt that this was basic not only to the establishment of programs, but to their perpetuation as well. Yet there was no felt need for education in Vicos and no value placed on educational attainment. There had never been any opportunity for nonagricultural employment, the former leasees had no interest in educating their laborers and possibly upsetting the status quo, and the teachers sent by the government were not only poorly trained but highly prejudicial towards the Indians. Thus in 1951 very few had ever attended school and only five people could be found who could read and write in even rudimentary fashion. So, community meetings were held, educational goals established, a new school built, and better teachers brought in. Incentives for school attendance included a free lunch program which helped to triple attendance in the first year.

All this was not accomplished without problems, however. People contributed their labor to build the school but remained suspicious of the outsiders' intentions, and some stole building materials. Again this was overcome through the medium of the town meeting and open discussion. The results of these educational efforts were quite dramatic. School attendance increased from a high of 18 in 1951 to 250 in 1958, and the number of teachers rose from 1 to 8 over the same period. In addition, an adult education program was initiated to provide literacy training for adults. This too met with considerable success. By the time the Cornell group pulled out, education had become a fully established value in Vicos. Parents cooperate in sending their children to school, show pride in their achievements, and participate in school activities and maintenance. Where the children are concerned their new skills have enabled them to enjoy new prestige at home and compete successfully in the outside world. This in turn has led to a more optimistic outlook for the future.

Similar progress was accomplished in the area of nutrition and health. More efficient agricultural techniques led to new and better crops with higher yields and even cash income. This, along with the school lunch program, led to a better diet and consequently improved nutrition. A clinic was established to provide health care twice weekly and as a result of this and the ready acceptance of modern medicine, infectuous diseases were largely eradicated.

The Cornell University lease terminated in 1957 and recomendations to transfer title to the people of Vicos met strong opposition. An absurdly high price was placed on the land and the program was labeled by some as a Communist plot and by others as a network of spies for the United States. So for five years the people of Vicos rented their own land with their own money. There was an understandable reluctance to continue the developmental programs since the people would lose the fruits of their labor should the land be put up for auction again. Then, in 1962, ten years after the Cornell project began at Vicos, the people were allowed to buy the land, in part due to diplomatic pressure exerted by the Kennedy Administration in Washington, for $74,000 on a time-payment plan.

Holmberg notes that the experience at Vicos shows that if granted respect, the Indian will give respect and that if allowed to share in the decision-making process he will take pride in making and carrying out decisions. Several of his associates conclude that:

The major lesson of Vicos, for Peru as a whole, is that its serf and suppressed peasant populations, once freed and given encouragement, technical assistance, and learning, can pull themselves up by their own bootstraps and become productive citizens of the nation. The Vicos experience also proved that this development did not require, in essence, vast investments of capital from outside sources. Rather it showed that with the appropriate opening of opportunity and strategic intervention from the outside (particularly technical assistance), such an impoverished and exploited community as the serfs of Vicos could actually finance, to a large degree, the changes necessary to provide for a greater sharing of human values.[11]

### SUMMARY

The anthropologist's role in directed change is examined in the beginning of this chapter and some of the problems encountered in directed-change programs are outlined. A model for evaluating such programs is presented and a number of factors which can influence the outcome of these programs are discussed. We then examined the saliency of these factors by considering the introduction of modern medicine into a Mayan Indian community. In this instance we concluded that a *felt need* for change along with evidence of practical benefit was sufficient to overcome a number of negative influences. We then looked at the Cornell-Vicos project of "participant intervention" as an example of a successful directed-change program. The Peruvian project provides a convenient prelude to our discussion of community development and modernization.

### For Further Reading

Arensberg, C. M. and A. H. Niehoff *Introducing Social Change.* Chicago: Aldine Publishing Company, 1964. A manual of practically applied change written specifically for the nonprofessional agent of change. A bit overladen with value judgements regarding the necessity of change.

Dobyns, H. F.; P. L. Doughty; and H. D. Laswell, eds. *Peasants, Power, and Applied Social Change: Vicos as a Model.* Beverly Hills: Sage Publications, 1964. The most complete published account of the "participant intervention" program of directed change in Vicos, Peru by Cornell University personnel. The authors underline the importance of the acquisition of power by developing groups as the key factor in successful development.

Foster, G. M. *Applied Anthropology.* Boston Houghton Mifflin Company, 1969. The best general work available on applied anthropology. Foster looks at the relationship between basic and applied research and assesses the anthropologist's role in applied change programs.

Niehoff, A. H. *A Casebook of Social Change.* Chicago: Aldine Publishing Company, 1966. A companion volume to the Arensberg and Niehoff book listed above. Here, a theoretical framework to evaluate change programs is presented and then actual accounts of changing projects from the five major developing areas of the world are considered.

Paul, B. D., ed. *Health, Culture, and Community.* New York: The Russell Sage Foundation, 1955. An excellent collection of essays on changing medical practices in various parts of the world with a general introduction and brief narrative throughout by the editor.

Spicer, E. H., ed. *Human Problems in Technological Change.* New York: The Russell Sage Foundation, 1952. A good selection of articles dealing with change presented in a standard format so that the reader can

11. Dobyns; Doughty; and Laswell, eds. *Peasants, Power and Applied Social Change: Vicos as a Model,* p. 61.

attempt to predict the consequences of each program. Spicer offers a few theoretical perspectives on applied change.

## Bibliography

Dobyns, H. F.; Doughty, P. L.; and Laswell, H. D., eds. 1964. *Peasants, Power, and Applied Change: Vicos as a Model.* Beverly Hills: Sage Publications.

Erasmus, C. J. 1961. *Man Takes Control: Cultural Development and American Aid.* New York: The Bobbs-Merrill Company.

Foster, G. M. 1962. *Traditional Cultures and the Impact of Technological Change.* New York: Harper & Row.

———. 1970. *Traditional Cultures and the Impact of Technological Change,* 2d. ed. New York: Harper & Row.

Goodenough, W. 1963. *Cooperation in Change: An Anthropological Approach to Community Development.* New York: The Russell Sage Foundation.

Holmberg, A. 1960. "Changing Community Values and Attitudes in Peru: A Case Study in Guided Change," Council on Foreign Relations, *Social Change in Latin America Today.* New York: Random House.

Kelly, I. 1960. *La Antropologia, la Cultura y la Salud Publica.* Lima, Peru: Imprenta del SCISP, Ministry of Public Health and Social Welfare.

Niehoff, A. H. 1966. *A Casebook of Social Change.* Chicago: Aldine Publishing Company.

Paul, B. D., ed. 1955. *Health, Culture, and Community.* New York: The Russell Sage Foundation.

Spicer, E. H., ed. 1952. *Human Problems in Technological Change.* New York: The Russell Sage Foundation.

Woods, C. M. 1970. "Medical Innovation in Highland Guatemala: The Case of San Lucas Tolimán." In *Stranger in Our Midst: Guided Culture Change in Highland Guatemala.* ed. P. Furst and K. Reed. Los Angeles: Latin American Center, University of California at Los Angeles.

# 6 | Community Development and Modernization

As the terms are used here, development refers to change at the community level and modernization to change at the individual level. The former can be defined as "the process whereby a contemporary society improves its control of the environment by means of an increasingly competent technology applied by increasingly complex organizations,"[1] and the latter as "the process by which individuals change from a traditional way of life to a more complex, technologically advanced and rapidly changing way of life."[2] Thus, in our example of directed change in Vicos, the input of capital, technology, health care, education, and new forms of sociopolitical organization constitute development while the adoption of these innovations by the people with consequent changes in life-styles constitutes modernization. A somewhat more comprehensive definition of modernization has been offered by Michael Robbins who sees this type of change as:

The process whereby an individual's patterns of behavior and culture changes from a traditional way of life oriented to the past and the present, to a more complex, technologically complicated and rapidly changing style of life oriented to the future, the antecedents of which are his increased exposure to and identification with: 1) residence and subsistence in urban areas; 2) formal education; 3) commercialization of land, labor, goods, and services; 4) a widening scale of social and cultural contacts, relations and involvements; 5) cosmopoliteness; 6) mass communication media; and 7) small and large-scale technological innovations.[3]

From these definitions we can pick out the following important characteristics of modernization. First, it is a process involving changes occurring over time in a wide variety of contexts; second, it is global in that it is taking place in most of the underdeveloped countries of the world; third, it refers specifically to individual change in contrast to community change; fourth, it is multidimensional in that it cannot be explained by single factors but rather by the interaction of multiple behaviors, attitudes, and forces; and fifth, it occurs at

1. T. Caplow and K. Finsterbusch, "Development Rank: A New Method of Rating National Development," Columbia University, Bureau of Applied Research. Quoted in Everett M. Rogers with Lynne Svenning, *Modernization Among Peasants: The Impact of Communication* (New York: Holt, Rinehart and Winston, 1969), p. 9.
2. Rogers with Svenning, *Modernization Among Peasants: The Impact of Communication,* p. 14.
3. Michael C. Robbins, "Modernization and Exploratory Behavior: An Example from Buganda," 1973, p. 5.

different rates both between and within different population clusters. These characteristics are partially summed up in Daniel Lerner's statement regarding the worldwide transformation from medieval to modern ways. The process he says

...worked itself out through millions of individual lives; many suffered, others prospered, while their world was being reshaped in the modern image. In the end, all men of the west had acquired a new style of life. A similar process is under way in the Middle East. But the process reaches different people in different settings and induces different dilemmas of personal choice.[4]

## THEORETICAL PERSPECTIVES

A number of "grand" theories have been proposed in attempting to account for the process of modernization. Most of these are based on single "prime movers" and generally combine modernization and development as a single force. We briefly mentioned the work of Max Weber in Chapter Three. He suggested that the growth of capitalism was dependent upon the acquisition of certain key social values associated with the Protestant Reformation and expressed in the Protestant Ethic. Positive attitudes towards hard work, thrift, savings, and upward social mobility supposedly led to economic development and modernization.[5]

Another theory, proposed by Walter Rostow, sees development and modernization occurring everywhere as a series of stages: (1) traditional society; (2) precondition for take-off; (3) take-off; (4) drive to maturity; and (5) high mass consumption. The "prime mover" here consists of a wide-spread desire for economic development arising during the take-off stage. This desire must then be recognized and acted upon by innovative entrepreneurs who lead the change effort.[6]

Everett Hagen places the roots of change in the sociopsychological processes of childhood personality development whereby two social values central to economic development are acquired. These values, autonomy and achievement, arise when some elite group in the traditional society suffers a loss of respect, status, and power through being conquered or deposed. Following a period of retreatism and inferiority the offspring of these fallen elites develop a high degree of autonomy and achievement motivation as a result of their nonauthoritarian upbringing. This generation then takes the lead in innovative activities and consequent economic growth.[7]

The work of David McClelland and Daniel Lerner is more empirically based but they too rely heavily on single causal factors. McClelland proposes "achievement motivation" as the crucial variable in individual impetus to change. This he defines as an inner concern with achievement, personal excellence, and self-accomplishment. His measure of this concept is based on historical documentation for the earlier periods of development and on psychological testing for the more contemporary periods. He found that traditional and peasant populations are generally low on achievement motivation because of blocked opportunities and exploitation. This leads to other sociopsychological characteristics which makes these groups unlikely candidates for mod-

4. Daniel Lerner, *The Passing of Traditional Society: Modernizing the Middle East* (New York: The Free Press, 1958), p. 43.

5. Max Weber, *The Protestant Ethic and the Spirit of Capitalism* (New York: Charles Scribner and Sons, 1953).

6. Walter W. Rostow, *The Stages of Economic Growth* (Cambridge: Cambridge University Press, 1960).

7. Everett E. Hagen, *On the Theory of Social Change: How Economic Growth Begins* (Homewood, Ill.: Dorsey Press, 1962).

ernization if left alone.[8] Instead of achievement motivation, Lerner relies on the notion of "empathy," which is defined as the ability to imagine one's self in the roles of others, as the crucial factor which sets off the modernization process. He interviewed 300 individuals in each of six Middle Eastern countries and found that those who rated high on empathy also tended to be more literate, urban, inclined to use the mass media, and generally nontraditional in orientation. He concludes that the acquisition and diffusion of empathy may well be the greatest characterological transformation in history and that it triggers modernization.

Everywhere...increasing urbanization has tended to raise literacy; rising literacy has tended to increase (mass) media exposure; increasing media exposure has 'gone with' wider economic participation (per capita income) and political participation (voting)...The same basic model reappears in virtually all modernizing societies on all continents of the world.[9]

Needless to say, Lerner is a bit prone to overstatement.

The most ambitious and systematic study of modernization published to date is that conducted by Everett Rogers and his associates.[10] Following an extensive review of the innovation literature Rogers launched an extensive study of modernization in five Columbian villages, some of which were more developed than others. The study is truly multidimensional in

that many variables are considered and an attempt is made to arrange them into a logical cause-and-effect sequence. Modernization is viewed essentially as a communication process with the underlying premise that "you have to find out about something before you can do it." The resulting model of modernization presented by Rogers is shown in Figure E. The main antecedents—literacy, exposure to the mass media, and a cosmopolite (urban) orientation—are said to lead to increased empathy (Lerner) and achievement motivation (McClelland), and decreased fatalism (the degree to which an individual perceives a lack of ability to control his own future). These sociopsychological characteristics then predispose people to innovate and increase both their political knowledge and aspirations for the future. In other words, the sociopsychological variables intervene between the antecedents which set off the modernization process and the consequences of that process —a more modern way of life. Now Rogers does not say this is the only ordering possible nor does he deny the possibility of feedback, that is, increased aspirations for

8. David C. McClelland, *The Achieving Society* (Princeton: Van Nostrand, 1961).
9. Lerner, *The Passing of Traditional Society: Modernizing the Middle East*, p. 46.
10. Rogers with Svenning, *Modernization Among Peasants: The Impact of Communication*.
11. Ibid., p. 50.

## FIGURE E

### EVERETT ROGERS, MODEL OF THE MODERNIZATION PROCESS[11]

| MAIN ANTECEDENTS → | INTERVENING VARIABLES → | MAIN CONSEQUENCES |
|---|---|---|
| Literacy | Empathy | Innovativeness |
| Media Exposure | Achievement Motivation | Political Knowledge |
| Cosmopoliteness | Low Fatalism | Aspirations |

the future could lead to higher achievement motivation which could then lead one to seek more education, and consequently, literacy. This particular model, or chain of events, simply seems to "fit" most favorably in terms of his data and logic. He considers alternate models and a number of other variables and compares his results with those of other studies. The multivariate nature of modernization comes through clearly in his analysis as he explains

the basic tenet is that the multitude of possible modernization concepts are connected in a cobweb of interdependent relationships, such that they function in a state of dynamic equilibrium. Variations in any one variable, therefore, trigger corresponding changes in numerous other concepts.[12]

He then concludes that

indeed, so many variables appear to be important parts of the modernization process that it is a formidable task to put them in some kind of order. In the process of probing the nature of modernization we now find ourselves unable to see the forest for the trees.[13]

Many students of community development and modernization subscribe to the theoretical assumption that the city is the basic source of innovation from which all change emanates. From this viewpoint development proceeds outward from urban centers so that communities further removed from the metropolis are less developed than those in closer contact with this source of innovation. This position is clearly evident in Robert Redfield's classic study of the "folk-urban continuum" in Yucatán, Mexico.[14] Redfield chose four communities which varied in size and complexity on a geographical continuum from the city of Merida on the coast to a remote village in the hinterland. The focus of the study was to define differences between isolated, homogeneous societies on

the one hand and mobile, heterogeneous societies on the other. With these differences established, he could then use the folk-urban continuum to show what happens when people from folk societies come into contact with the people and influences of urban societies. The folk society is characterized as

...small, isolated, non-literate, and homogeneous, with a strong sense of group solidarity. The ways of living are conventionalized into that coherent system which we call 'a culture.' Behavior is traditional, spontaneous, uncritical, and personal; there is no legislation or habit of experiment and reflection for intellectual ends. Kinship, its relationships and institutions, are the type categories of experience and the familial group is the unit of action. The sacred prevails over the secular; the economy is one of status rather than the market.[15]

The urban end of the continuum is not explicitly defined but Redfield clearly implies a variant of Euro-American culture and society and represents life in the city as more or less the polar opposite of that in the folk village. He concludes that as one moves along the continuum from folk to urban, cultural disorganization, secularization, and individualism increase. This is accompanied by commercialism and individual anxiety and insecurity.

Others have shown that this is not always the case. Referring to the communities situated on Lake Atitlán in highland Guatemala (see page 29) Sol Tax states that

...a stable society can be small, unsophisticated, homogeneous in beliefs and practices ...[and yet have]...relationships impersonal, with formal institutions dictating the

12. Rogers with Svenning, *Modernization Among Peasants: The Impact of Communication*, p. 316.
13. Ibid.
14. Robert Redfield, *The Folk Culture of Yucatan* (Chicago: University of Chicago Press, 1941).
15. Ibid., p. 293.

acts of individuals, with familial organization weak, with life secularized, and with individuals acting more from economic or other personal advantage than from any deep conviction or thought of the social good.[16]

It has also been pointed out that in West Africa there are many large urban communities which exhibit complex economic specialization, the use of money, and profit motivation but whose social relations are as personal as those in Redfield's folk societies and where religion is the focal aspect of the culture. In other words, these constitute folk *sacred* societies.[17] Finally, in a study of Timbuctoo, French West Africa, Horace Minor has shown that "...this densely populated, heterogeneous, non-isolated community showed social disorganization and was characterized by secular behavior and impersonal relationships, even in the *absence* of influences from Western civilization."[18] [emphasis added]

In addition to these, and other, exceptions which show that disorganization, secularization, and individualism need not accompany nor necessarily be caused by urban influences, the validity of the folk-urban continuum has been questioned on a number of other grounds. These include the emphasis on the city as the sole source of change, Redfield's obvious idealization of folk culture, the lack of substantiating psychological data, and the reliance upon ideal types.[19] In spite of these criticisms, however, the "folk-urban continuum" if used with appropriate caution affords some important theoretical and methodological guidelines for the study of change and has resulted in some productive research efforts.[20]

Drawing on ethnographic information gathered in various parts of the world, but primarily Latin America, Frank Young and his associates have constructed various scales in an attempt to explicate the content and direction of community development.[21] From these, they have offered some generalizations regarding the developmental process. These include: (1) communities develop according to a cumulative unidimensional sequence; (2) this sequence holds for communities of all sizes and all cultures; (3) the degree and intensity of development is directly proportionate to the amount of communication with the outside world; (4) the direction of community growth is always toward greater participation in the national social structure; and (5) the population size of the community increases in direct proportion to the degree of development.[22] These generalizations, and the methodology used to establish them, have been subjected to considerable criticism.[23] The no-

16. Sol Tax, "Culture and Civilization in Guatemalan Societies," *Scientific Monthly* 48 (1939):467.

17. Melville J. Herskovitz, *Cultural Dynamics* (New York: Alfred A. Knopf, 1947), p. 220.

18. Horace Minor, "The Folk-Urban Continuum," in *Social Change: Sources, Patterns, and Consequences*, A. Etzioni and E. Etzioni, eds. (New York: Basic Books, 1964), p. 149.

19. Oscar Lewis, *Life in a Mexican Village: Tepoztlan Restudied* (Urbana: University of Illinois Press, 1951).

20. Minor, "The Folk-Urban Continuum," in *Social Change: Sources, Patterns, and Consequences*, A. Etzioni and E. Etzioni, pp. 147-58.

21. See, especially, Frank W. Young and Isao Fujimoto, "Social Differentiation in Latin American Communities," *Economic Development and Cultural Change* 13 (1965):344-52; Frank W. Young and Ruth Young, "Toward a Theory of Community Development," in *The Challenge of Development*, R. J. Ward, ed. (Chicago: Aldine, 1967); and Frank W. Young, Berkeley A. Spencer and Jan L. Flora, "Differentiation and Solidarity in Agricultural Communities," *Human Organization* 27 (1968):344-51.

22. Young and Young, "Toward a Theory of Community Development" in *The Challenge of Development*, R. J. Ward, ed. (Chicago: Aldine, 1967).

23. Theodore D. Graves, Nancy B. Graves, and Michael J. Kobrin, "Historical Inferences from Guttman Scales: The Return of Age-Area Magic?" *Current Anthropology* 10 (1969):317-38.

tion that the developmental sequence is the same everywhere (generalizations one and two) smacks of the unilineal emphasis proposed by the classical evolutionists discussed in chapter one and is open to similar criticism. While these propositions may have limited application on a regional basis, the expectation that they will hold on a worldwide basis is doubtful—if not ridiculous. Generalizations three and four are generally confirmed by the anthropological literature but must still be taken with caution. Finally, while population growth is closely related to development (generalization five), it cannot be shown that population increases in *direct* proportion to community development. The fact that even simple generalizations like these do not hold up consistently under systematic testing serves to underscore one of the lingering problems facing students of change today. In spite of several generations of intensive research we still face a paucity of established, testable theory regarding sociocultural change.

In an attempt to further clarify the processes involved in community development and modernization, and to consider some of the theoretical statements reviewed above, we will turn to an ongoing study of change in the midwestern highlands of Guatemala. To place this project in appropriate perspective, however, we should briefly consider the ways in which anthropologists go about studying, or measuring, change.

### APPROACHES TO THE STUDY OF CHANGE

There are four basic approaches used by anthropologists to study sociocultural change: historical reconstruction, cross-sectional analysis, the study-restudy, and longitudinal analysis. Commonly, two or more of these approaches are used concur-

rently as they compliment one another and offer further insight into the change process. *Historical reconstruction* relies on written materials, the archaeological record, and where possible, informant recall, to reconstruct the past. Most of our information on American Indians has been gathered in this way, particularly through intensive and exhaustive interviews with older members of a given tribe who are able to recount their own experiences and those passed down to them from their forebears. The evolutionists and diffusionists discussed earlier relied on historical reconstruction—and a goodly amount of imagination and fantasy—as did Lauriston Sharp in his account of the Yir Yiront, and Murphy and Steward in their description of parallel acculturation among rubber tappers and fur trappers. The major problem with this approach is that the investigator must rely on the authenticity of historical documents and on the ability of key informants to accurately recall and report the past.

*Cross-sectional analysis* is probably the most popular current approach applied to study change. This involves using the range of variation in behavior, belief, and attitude existent in a society at one point in time to *infer* the process of change. For example, the Menomini Indians studied by the Spindlers were grouped into different categories on the basis of social, cultural, and psychological indicators. From this information one can infer that the "native-oriented" Menomini will eventually move through the "transitional" categories to one of the "acculturated types"—in other words, this appears to be the way change is going on in Menomini society. In Adams' study of change in Guatemalan Indian communities we assume that "traditional" Indian communities will become "modified" and then "Ladinoized," and in Woods' study of individual acculturation we can infer that these Mayan Indians will eventually all shed their native dress, language, housing, and customs to become more like their Ladino counterparts. Rogers' study of modernization in Columbia is also cross-sectional—the data was collected at one point in time and the range of variation on the many variables is used to infer the process of modernization. It should be emphasized, however, that people and groups do not necessarily follow one another through exactly similar paths of change—and this is *implied* in cross-sectional analysis. Any number of events may retard, accelerate, or even completely reverse the way changes are occurring in a given society.

The *study-restudy* is a little used but potentially valuable method for the study of change. This involves returning to a previously studied society and conducting a restudy. Ideally, but seldom, the same investigator undertakes both the before and after investigations. This was the case in Margaret Mead's previously reported work with the Manus in the South Pacific. Time *one* can be compared with time *two* to see what changes have taken place. Note, however, that this approach can yield information only on *what* has changed. One must still rely on inference to explain *why* and *how* these changes took place—that is, the actual process of change, Of course, historical reconstruction can be used to aid in this endeavor. A more serious limitation of this approach is that commonly two different investigators conduct the two studies. Since they may well differ in theoretical orientation, kind of data collected, and how this information is interpreted, many sources of error are possible. A classic example of this problem can be seen in Oscar Lewis' restudy of a village in Mexico some fifteen years after it was studied by his former professor, Robert Redfield.[24] Redfield had characterized Tepoztlán as a relatively

homogeneous, isolated, smoothly functioning, and well-integrated society made up of contented and well-adjusted people (recall Redfield's idealization of the "folk" society presented earlier in this chapter). Lewis, on the other hand, describes the uncooperativeness, tension, factionalism, maliciousness, and strained interpersonal relationships in the same village. Both men agreed that these differences were not due to changes during the fifteen-year period between their respective studies. Redfield ascribed the conflicting reports to differing interests while Lewis suggested that Redfield simply conducted sloppy fieldwork and misinterpreted what he saw. Perhaps the best example of the study-restudy apprach is Raymond Firth's work with the Tikopia in the Solomon Islands.[25]

The *longitudinal* study of change allows the best opportunity for an accurate account of the what, why, and how of change but has seldom been used because of the great committment in time, effort, and money such an approach requires. Similar kinds of information must be gathered on the same group using similar methods at regular intervals over an extended period of time—or, the observations may be continuous. The only real longitudinal study of change which has been reported in anthropological literature to any extent is the Cornell/Vicos project outlined above. In this case, a team of researchers conducted continuing observances on the same group as they made the relatively rapid transition from dependent serfs to autonomous and relatively independent land owners. Since multiple changes were actually introduced by the same people con-

---

24. See, Robert Redfield, *Tepoztlan: A Mexican Village* (Chicago: University of Chicago Press, 1930) and Lewis, *Life in a Mexican Village: Tepoztlán Restudied.*
25. Raymond Firth, *Social Change in Tikopia, Restudy of a Polynesian Community After a Generation* (London: George Allen and Unwin, 1959).

ducting the investigation, this project provided a unique opportunity for the study of change.

## SUMMARY

The purpose of this chapter was to present the general dimensions of community development and modernization as a prelude to the more detailed consideration of change in one region. This follows in the next chapter. We distinguished between development and modernization and reviewed a number of studies which attempted to explain these kinds of changes. We also examined the folk-urban continuum which proposes the city as the major source of change and discussed some theoretical propositions regarding development. Where modernization is concerned, we emphasized that this is a complex process and multivariate in nature. The chapter concludes with a discussion of how anthropologists approach the study of change.

### For Further Reading

Chodak, S. *Societal Development: Five Approaches with Conclusions From Comparative Analysis.* New York: Oxford University Press, 1973. Chodak reviews much of the literature on societal development, compares findings, and suggests some new directions.

Dalton, G., ed. *Economic Development and Social Change: The Modernization of Village Communities.* Garden City, New York: The Natural History Press, 1971. A collection of twenty-eight essays by anthropologists, economists, historians, and sociologists which treat many dimensions of change in the underdeveloped areas of the world. A lengthy introduction by the editor places the material in appropriate perspective.

Geertz, C., ed. *Old Societies and New States: The Quest for Modernity in Asia and Africa.* New York: The Free Press, 1963. A good collection of essays on modernization in Asia and Africa compiled and introduced by one of the better informed experts on this topic. Some emphasis on ethnic and political perspectives in modernization.

Hagen, E. E. *On the Theory of Social Change: How Economic Growth Begins.* Homewood, Illinois: The Dorsey Press, 1962. Although Hagen's central thesis concerning personality change and development is highly debatable, he presents a wealth of descriptive materials on the developing nations.

Hunter, G. *Modernizing Peasant Societies.* New York: Oxford University Press, 1969. A sensible and relatively comprehensible treatment of modernization placed within the author's own theoretical perspective. Emphasis on materials from India.

Rogers, E. M. with L. Svenning *Modernization Among Peasants: The Impact of Communication.* New York: Holt, Rinehart and Winston, 1969. The most systematic and comprehensive study of regional modernization published to date. Rogers and associates collected a vast array of data on individuals in five Columbian communities in an attempt to measure relevant variables in the modernization process. An attempt is also made to place these variables in a logical sequence.

### Bibliography

Caplow, T. and Finsterbusch, K. 1964. "A New Method of Rating National Development." Columbia University, Bureau of Applied Social Research.

Firth, R. 1959. *Social Change in Tikopia: Restudy of a Polynesian Community After a Generation.* London: George Allen and Unwin.

Graves, T. D.; Graves N. B.; and Kobrin, M. J. 1969. "Historical Inferences from Guttman

Scales: The Return of Age Area Magic?"
*Current Anthropology* 10: 317-338.

Hagen, E. E. 1962. *On the Theory of Social Change: How Economic Growth Begins* Homewood, Ill.: The Dorsey Press.

Herskovitz, M. J. 1947. *Cultural Dynamics.* New York: Alfred A. Knopf.

Lerner, D. 1958. *The Passing of Traditional Society: Modernizing the Middle East.* New York: The Free Press.

Lewis, O. 1951. *Life in a Mexican Village: Tepoztlan Restudied.* Urbana: University of Illinois Press.

McClelland, D. C. 1961. *The Achieving Society.* Princeton, N.J.: Van Nostrand.

Minor, H. 1964. "The Folk-Urban Continuum." In *Social Change: Sources, Patterns, and Consequences* ed. A. Etzioni and E. Etzioni. New York: Basic Books Inc., pp. 147-158.

Redfield, R. 1930. *Tepoztlan: A Mexican Village.* Chicago: University of Chicago Press.

————. 1941. *The Folk Culture of Yucatan.* Chicago: University of Chicago Press.

Robbins, M. C. 1973. "Modernization and Exploratory Behavior: An Example from Buganda."

Rogers, E. M. with Svenning, L. 1969. *Modernization Among Peasants: The Impact of Communication.* New York: Holt, Rinehart, and Winston.

Rostow, W. W. 1960. *The Stages of Economic Growth: A Non-Communist Manifesto.* London: Cambridge University Press.

Tax, S. 1939. "Culture and Civilization in Guatemalan Societies." *Scientific Monthly* 48: 463-467.

Young, F. W. and Fujimoto, I. 1965. "Social Differentiation in Latin American Communities." *Economic Development and Cultural Change* 13: 344-352.

Young, F. W. and Young, R. 1967. "Toward a Theory of Community Development." In *The Challenge of Development* ed. R. J. Ward. Chicago: Aldine Publishing Company.

Young, F. W.; Spencer, B. A.; Flora, J. L. 1968. "Differentiation and Solidarity in Agricultural Communities." *Human Organization* 27: 344-351.

Weber, M. 1953. *The Protestant Ethic and the Spirit of Capitalism.* New York: Charles Scribner and Sons.

# 7 | Change in Highland Guatemala

The Guatemalan Research Project, initiated and directed by this writer, is a longitudinal study of change. It is focused on the Mayan towns which surround Lake Atitlán in the midwestern highlands.[1] (See map page 63.) As previously described (see page 29), these towns share a common cultural tradition but exhibit a number of significant differences from one to the other. These differences, along with differential exposure to change influences and varying community reaction to these, make this particular region an ideal natural laboratory for the study of sociological change. The basic research strategy involves the collection of a wide range of social, cultural, and psychological data on samples of individuals and families in a series of communities at stipulated intervals over an extended period of time. This data is complemented by a comprehensive "attribute survey" designed to measure exposure, development, and traditionality at the community level at similar intervals of time. The design of the research allows the measurement of individual and community change at different points in time so that individual change (modernization) can be compared with community change (development). Variable change influences, and their effects can be recorded and those areas most or least resistant to change can be located.[2]

As illustrated in Figure F the methodology also allows for intrasociety and intersociety cross-sectional analyses at each interval of time. That is, we can look at the range of variability on various traits in society A, B, C, and so on in an attempt to infer the process of change within these communities at one point in time and we can look at the range of variability exhibited from one town to the next in an attempt to infer the process of change between communities. What we end up with is a continuum of individual change, or modernization, within and between communities and a continuum of community change, or development, from one community to the

1. The project is conducted each summer by faculty and students of the Department of Anthropology, University of California at Los Angeles. Given this limited research period each year we are still in the early stages of our work. In 1969 and 1970 we began by drafting and pretesting basic interview and attribute schedules. These were revised and administered in 1971 and 1972—the attribute survey was conducted in fourteen towns and the individual interview schedule was administered to random samples in ten of these. During 1973 and 1974 we continued to observe the change situation although no systematic efforts were undertaken. These will be resumed in 1975 and 1976.

2. Support for the project is provided by departmental research funds, the Latin American Center, UCLA, and the National Institute of Mental Health (MH 10576 and MH 23285).

CULTURE CHANGE
*Change in Highland Guatemala*

next. The models of change which result from these cross-sectional analyses can then be checked for accuracy by adding the longitudinal perspective. That is, we can compare our static models of change from Time One to Time Two to Time Three and so forth to see if our inferences about the process of change are correct. This can best be clarified by some concrete examples. First we will look at community development. Then we will compare development and modernization and, finally, examine the process of change within specific towns. This should provide a better understanding of both community development and modernization and, in addition, shed further light on the dynamics of sociocultural change in general.

### COMMUNITY DEVELOPMENT

In order to examine relevant relationships it is first necessary to arrange the towns in developmental order. Although there are more precise statistical procedures which could be used to accomplish this, we will rely on a straightforward system of rankings. It should be noted in passing, however, that alternative measures of each variable to be considered have been constructed and these reveal the same ordering. Our measure of relative community development is based on the presence or absence of twenty-seven traits ranging from corn mill, small store, and resident nurse which all towns have, to hotel, taxi, and pool hall which only one town has. The resulting developmental continuum is shown in Figure G. As we move from right to left the towns are less developed because as we move from top to bottom we see that they have a lower frequency and less complex array of the developmental indicators.

Now this is a cross-sectional analysis in that we have used the range of variability of these traits within the lake region at one point in time to construct a developmental continuum. From this we can *infer*, albeit cautiously, the process of development occurring in this area. For example, we suspect that as Santa Cruz develops it will get a bar, water in the houses, a butcher shop, and so on. Similarly, Santiago

## FIGURE F

### MODEL FOR THE STUDY OF CHANGE IN HIGHLAND GUATEMALA

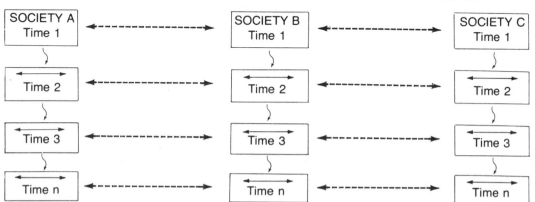

The solid lines within the boxes represent intrasociety variation, the broken lines represent intersociety variation, and the wavy lines represent change over time.

should get a secondary school and San Lucas a hotel. A number of things might effect this developmental sequence, however, and that is why we must exercise caution in our inferences. Demographic changes could result in the loss of traits once present, government programs could accelerate the rate of development in some towns, and geographical barriers may prohibit the entrance of some traits.

**FIGURE G**

### DEVELOPMENT IN TEN LAKE TOWNS

| | Panajachel | San Lucas | Santiago | San Pedro | San Juan | San Pablo | San Antonio | San Marcos | Santa Catarina | Santa Cruz |
|---|---|---|---|---|---|---|---|---|---|---|
| *RANKS* | | | | | | | | | | |
| Development | 1 | 2 | 3 | 4 | 5 | 6 | 7 | 8 | 9 | 10 |
| Exposure | 1 | 2 | 3 | 4 | 6 | 5 | 7 | 8 | 9 | 10 |
| Traditionality (−) | 2 | 3 | 5 | 1 | 4 | 7 | 6 | 9 | 8 | 10 |
| Population | 4 | 2 | 1 | 3 | 7 | 5 | 6 | 9 | 8 | 10 |
| *INDICATORS* | | | | | | | | | | |
| Corn Mill | + | + | + | + | + | + | + | + | + | + |
| Small Store | + | + | + | + | + | + | + | + | + | + |
| Resident Nurse | + | + | + | + | + | + | + | + | + | + |
| Bar | + | + | + | + | + | + | + | + | + | |
| Water in Houses | + | + | + | + | + | − | + | + | + | |
| Butcher Shop | + | + | + | + | + | + | + | + | | |
| Overnight Lodging | + | + | + | + | + | + | + | + | | |
| Boat Service | + | + | + | + | + | + | + | | | |
| Bakery | + | + | + | + | + | − | + | | | |
| Resident Pastor | + | + | + | + | + | + | | | | |
| Tailor Shop | + | + | + | + | + | + | | | | |
| Carpenter Shop | + | + | + | + | + | + | | | | |
| Road | + | + | + | + | + | | | | | |
| Coffee Ranch | + | + | + | + | + | | | | | |
| Cafe | + | + | + | + | + | | | | | |
| Doctor Visits | + | + | + | + | | | | | | |
| Room and Board | + | + | + | + | | | | | | |
| Resident Priest | + | + | + | + | | | | | | |
| Resident Doctor | + | + | + | | | | | | | |
| Gas Station | + | + | + | | | | | | | |
| National Police | + | + | + | | | | | | | |
| Seconday School | + | + | | | | | | | | |
| Auto Repair | + | + | | | | | | | | |
| Boat Yard | + | + | | | | | | | | |
| Hotel | + | | | | | | | | | |
| Taxi | + | | | | | | | | | |
| Pool Hall | + | | | | | | | | | |

Plus = Trait Present
Minus = Trait Absent

The introduction of electricity, for example, did not follow this sequence. Towns which voted for the winning political party over the years got electricity first,[3] followed by adjoining towns closest to the main power lines. These towns, though, had to raise a considerable sum of money to offset installation costs and this required a community vote. In addition, some towns had already financed independent electric plants and chose to rely on these. So, electricity entered Panajachel, San Pedro, Santa Catarina, and San Lucas in that order. Since these data were collected in 1972 several new roads have been built and this does not quite follow our sequence. In 1973 the road was extended from San Juan to San Pablo and from Panajachel to Santa Catarina—and it should have reached San Antonio in late 1974. The road should extend to San Marcos some time in 1975 but Santa Cruz, because of the rough terrain, cannot be reached by a lakeside road and will have to await connection with the towns 2000 feet above the lake. Santa Catarina got its electricity and road out of sequence because of its proximity to Panajachel (refer to the map on page 63). Another problem with our continuum is that San Pablo does not have running water in the houses nor a bakery as we would expect. On the other hand, there are plans for a hotel in San Lucas, Santa Cruz got its bar and Santiago its secondary school in 1974, and the lights went on in San Juan and San Pablo simultaneously in mid-September of the same year.

The towns, in Figure G, are also ranked on relative population size, exposure to change influences, and degree of traditionality. According to the theories of development we mentioned previously we might expect the more developed towns to be larger, more exposed, and less traditional. These propositions are largely supported by the data although the correlations are not perfect. This can be explained. The population rankings, based on projections from the 1964 national census, indicate that larger populations go along with development but are definitely not *directly* proportionate to one another. The three least developed towns all have populations below 1,000 while the towns in the middle ranges run from 1,500 to 2,200 people. Of the four most developed towns, Panajachel is the smallest with about 3,500 and Santiago the largest with over 12,000 inhabitants. These figures suggest that development requires a relatively large population but that once a certain level is reached, other factors have more affect on the rate and degree of development.

Certainly exposure is the most important of these and this is supported by the near perfect correlation between the two rankings. The exposure ranking is based on the number of buses and passenger boats available weekly, the percentage of Ladinos and Protestants in the populations, the number of newspapers received weekly, and relative isolation. Buses, boats, and newspapers allow increased contact with the outside world while Ladinos afford the Indians with a first-hand model of the more modern way of life. Conversion to Protestantism, as mentioned above, automatically tears the Indians away from many of their traditional practices and beliefs. The fact that San Pablo ranks higher than San Juan on exposure probably reflects the fact that it has the second largest relative Protestant population on the lake. Compared to some

3. The writer accompanied town government officials from San Lucas to the second largest city in the republic in 1966 where they drew up and signed a formal agreement with the National Institute of Electricity and one of the political parties which stipulated that if the town voted with that particular party and the party won, San Lucas would get electricity. The party lost and San Lucas waited another seven years for lights.

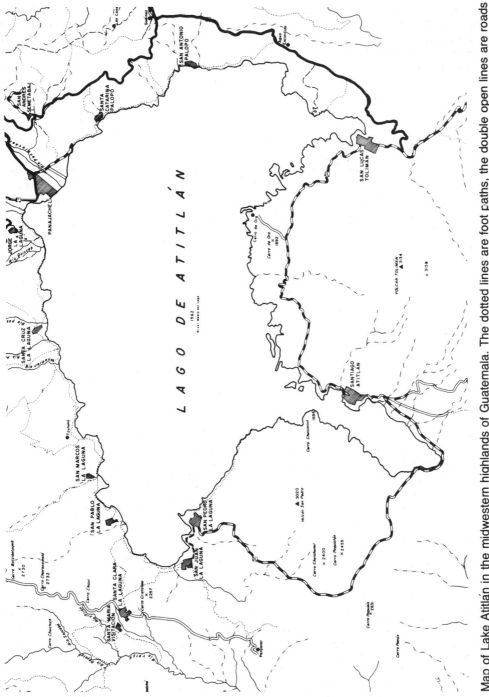

Map of Lake Atitlán in the midwestern highlands of Guatemala. The dotted lines are foot paths, the double open lines are roads passable only during the dry season, the double spaced lines are all-weather, nonpaved roads, and the solid lines are paved roads. The lake is 5,100 feet high and roughly 12 miles long. Adapted from Sol Tax, ed., Los Pueblos del Lago Atitlán. Guatemala: Seminario de Integracion Social, 1968.

of the other towns, however, San Pablo has been a "late starter" in terms of development.

The ranks on traditionality are reversed so as to correspond with the others—the lower numbers represent less traditionality and the higher more. Traditionality is measured by the number of positions in the religious hierarchy, respected elders (men who have reached the top of the civil-religious hierarchy), sweat baths, and traditional curers in each town relative to population size. The correlation with development is respectable—the most developed towns show the least traditionality—although Santiago, and particularly San Pedro, do not fit well into the expected pattern. This requires explanation. Where Santiago is concerned, population size is probably the best explanation. This town is more than twice the size of any other town on the lake so that in spite of considerable economic input, communication, and exposure, it retains a large traditional population segment. All the women wear distinctive community dress as do most of the men. Over 90 percent of the residence plots have sweat baths, the civil-religious hierachy remains the most viable on the lake, and the native curers are so well known that they are visited by people from the entire region. So at least in this case, it would appear that development need not destroy important traditional patterns of living—at least not in the early stages. This apparent anomaly is even more dramatic when we consider that Santiago is visited every day of the year by a special tourist boat, has a resident Catholic mission sponsoring manifold change projects including such things as a radio station, and is the only town on the lake with a hospital.

San Pedro presents a somewhat different anomaly. It lies in the middle of the developmental spectrum but ranks as the least traditional town on the lake. Fortu-nately, San Pedro has been studied over a thirty-five year period so that considerable information is available to offer an explanation for this situation.[4] First of all, the people in San Pedro have always been known for their industry and entrepreneurial activities. They conduct commercial activities in many parts of the republic and have managed to purchase a good portion of the land in neighboring San Juan over the years—with the result that people from San Juan now find themselves working for Pedranos on land which was once their own. This accounts in part for San Pedro's fairly high rank on development. Related to this, and bearing on the low degree of traditionality, is the fact that over 50 percent of San Pedro's population of 4,500 are Protestants and another 30 percent have joined reformed Catholicism. These and other factors, which will be outlined in more detail below, have led to the collapse of the religious hierarchy in San Pedro with the resulting loss of the many traditional patterns of belief and behavior which accompany this institution. San Pedro is the only town on the lake without religious fraternities. Ladino influence is almost non-existent within the town, however, as they account for only about 1 percent of the population. And, as Ben Paul, who knows the Pedranos best, has explained it, the Ladinos in San Pedro tend to blend into the Indian life-style rather than vice versa.

4. See, for example, Sol Tax, *The Towns of Lake Atitlán*. Microfilm Collection on Middle American Cultural Anthropology, no. 13 (Chicago: University of Chicago Library, 1946) and Benjamin D. Paul, "San Pedro la Laguna" in Los Pueblos del Lago Atitlán, Sol Tax, ed. (Guatemala: Seminario de Integracion Social, 1968). Juan de Dios Rosales also conducted extensive research in San Pedro beginning in 1938 but to the best of this writer's knowledge the results have not been formally published.

We could recount many other exceptions and peculiarities occurring in the area as development proceeds. The major point to be made, however, is that in spite of our attempts to clarify through generalization, there are any number of factors which effect the change process so that blanket statements simply cannot be made. There are many alternative paths to development and it is doubtful if any single scheme can be used to account for it—even on a limited regional basis. Similar statements can be made about the modernization process to which we now turn.

### DEVELOPMENT AND MODERNIZATION

Modernization has been previously defined as a process whereby individuals change from a traditional to a more complex, technologically advanced, and rapidly changing life-style. We shall look at selected aspects of this process in two communities after an examination of the relationship between development and modernization in six of the towns on the developmental continuum. We will rely

again on a simple ranking procedure. As shown in Figure H the six towns selected for comparison are ranked again on development, exposure, traditionality, and population size at the community level. Then, data collected on random samples of individuals within each town is used to rank the towns on eight variables of assummed importance in the modernization process.[5] The rankings in this case are

5. Measurement of the modernization variables is based on the following—*Economics*: Cash value of residence plot, house, land, and last crop; *Innovation*: Type of dress, household possesions, and religious preferences; *Traditionalism*: Level of service in the religious fraternities, preference for further service, and use of traditional curers; *Fatalism*: Response to ten questions which measure one's feeling of control over his own destiny; *Household Construction*: Materials used in building primary structure; *Traditional Beliefs*: Acceptance or rejection of ten traditional beliefs: *Literacy*: Combined scores for tests on reading, writing, and Spanish facility; and *Political Knowledge*: Responses to fourteen questions regarding local, national, and international political events. The ranks on traditionalism, fatalism, and traditional beliefs have been reversed so as to correspond with the other rankings where the lower rank indicates relatively more modernity.

### FIGURE H

#### DEVELOPMENT AND MODERNIZATION IN SIX LAKE TOWNS

| | DEVELOPMENT | | | | MODERNIZATION | | | | | | | |
|---|---|---|---|---|---|---|---|---|---|---|---|---|
| | Development | Exposure | Traditionality (↑) | Population | Economics | Innovation | Traditionalism (↑) | Fatalism (↑) | Household Construction | Traditional Beliefs (↑) | Literacy | Political Knowledge |
| Panajachel | 1 | 1 | 2 | 4 | 1 | 1 | 3 | 2 | 2 | 2 | 1 | 3 |
| San Lucas | 2 | 2 | 3 | 2 | 2 | 3 | 1 | 3 | 5 | 4 | 5 | 4 |
| Santiago | 3 | 3 | 5 | 1 | 4 | 5 | 4 | 4 | 3 | 5 | 6 | 5 |
| San Pedro | 4 | 4 | 1 | 3 | 3 | 2 | 2 | 1 | 1 | 1 | 4 | 1 |
| San Juan | 5 | 5 | 4 | 5 | 5 | 4 | 5 | 5 | 4 | 3 | 2 | 2 |
| San Marcos | 6 | 6 | 6 | 6 | 6 | 6 | 6 | 6 | 6 | 6 | 3 | 6 |

based on the mean, or average, scores registered by the samples from each town. In scanning all the comparative rankings, which are arranged in order of closest correspondence with the developmental continuum from left to right, it is clear that there is not a one-to-one relationship between development and modernization. It would appear, however, that the discrepancies which show up may well be due to the same anomalies we discovered in explaining the developmental continuum—Santiago and San Pedro. To review in brief, Santiago is high on development and exposure, but due to its size retains a fairly large traditional population component. This is clearly reflected on the individual rankings as Santiago scores lower on modernization across the board relative to development. Only on household construction does it equal its developmental rank. San Pedro, on the other hand, reveals its progressive nature by its very high scores on modernization relative to development.

San Juan also ranks relatively high on a number of the modernization variables. This is probably due to its proximity and ties with San Pedro along with fairly large Protestant and reformed Catholic population. Economic level, as might be expected, is almost perfectly correlated with community development—again, only San Pedro is out of order—suggesting that input at the community level is reflected in economic advance at the individual level. Community level traditionality also corresponds fairly well with individual traditionality. All in all, we will have to conclude that development and modernization in this Guatemalan case do not show consistent associations one with the other. Considering the anomalies presented by San Pedro and Santiago, however, the data seem more reasonable. Community change and individual change are associated, but not perfectly—they can proceed at somewhat different rates and lag can occur in either one.

In considering only the modernization variables quite a bit more consistency is apparent. While far from perfect, the ranks across the towns are fairly close. This provides some evidence that the various behaviors, beliefs, and attitudes indicative of modernization change at similar rates although again some lag is obvious. That this correspondence is not perfect is expected. We need only recall Everett Rogers' warning that it remains a formidable task to place the many modernization variables in some kind of logical order and that, where the process of modernization is concerned, the trees still obscure the forest.

Our final efforts will be directed towards investigating how and why change occurs focusing on particular communities. In San Lucas we will consider modernization with particular reference to medical changes, and in San Pedro we will look at the multiple factors which led to the downfall of the religious fraternities.

## MEDICAL CHANGE IN SAN LUCAS TOLIMAN

In considering the processes of change we pointed out that changes usually come in groups, are commonly linked in a sequence whereby acceptance of one may well lead to acceptance of another so that change tends to breed further change, and that some people adopt changes sooner than others. Now if we combine these basic notions with the fact that change is a constant in all sociocultural systems, we would expect to find a certain degree of individual variability in belief and behavior in all societies at any given point of time. And, this variability will be greater in societies undergoing relatively rapid change. We have shown above that this variation within a society can be used to illustrate the process of change. Similar procedures will be followed in demonstrating the process of change in San Lucas. Considerable background information on this town has been presented in previous chapters (see pages 32-35).

The basic thrust of this writer's research in San Lucas was to investigate changing medical practices and beliefs. This town was selected for such a study because modern medicine had only recently been introduced into the community and a number of other changes were already taking place. In short, a dynamic environment of change was apparent. The medical situation was particularly interesting since modern medicine joined the existing folk Ladino and folk Indian curing traditions to create a circumstance whereby competing, and often mutually inconsistent, curing strategies were offerred to the native population. Ladinos, by the way, even though they have their own folk practitioners, had been using nonresident modern medical practitioners for some time. So here too, the Ladino population presents the Indian with a model of the more modern way of life—the use of modern medicine.

Some of the findings from this research can be summarily discussed. Of particular importance is the sequence of change which is occurring in the community. This is shown in Figure I. This model of the change process is based on statistical procedures and multiple measures of all the variables. These will not be discussed here. It should be noted, however, that this is an "ideal" model just as others we have discussed. According to the qualitative and quantitative evidence available it would appear that a sizeable group of people in San Lucas are following this particular sequence of change. Other routes

to modernization are also possible and, as emphasized many times the process of change need not be unidirectional—feedback must be taken into account.

As presented, the model suggests that involvement in the cash economy leads to increased exposure to the outside world which in turn favors individual innovativeness. This propensity to innovate is also reflected in changing medical practices and since many of these practices tend to conflict with traditional beliefs they begin to disappear. We can briefly elaborate on this particular path to change. Involvement in the cash economy requires wage labor, entrepreneurial activity, or the production of surplus products for sale. This links the Indian with the regional and, to some extent, the national economy and involves varying degrees of exposure to the outside world. By contrast, one who devotes himself to traditional subsistence agricultural pursuits can avoid most contact with the changing world around him. He spends his time working his own land and disposes of whatever surplus he may have through local markets or middlemen. His own modest market purchases are conducted in local markets and primarily by his wife.

On the other hand, exposure to people and ideas outside the local community fosters a predisposition to innovate. These are the people who are most likely to change to

6. Adapted from Clyde M. Woods and Theodore D. Graves, *The Process of Medical Change in the Highland Guatemalan Town.* Latin American Center, University of California (1973), p. 51.

## FIGURE I

### MODEL OF THE CHANGE PROCESS IN SAN LUCAS TOLIMAN[6]

| CASH ECONOMY | → | EXPOSURE | → | INNOVATIVE NESS | → | MEDICAL PRACTISES | → | TRADITIONAL BELIEFS |
|---|---|---|---|---|---|---|---|---|

modern dress, reject further service in the civil-religious hierarchy, have a legally sanctioned union, build an outhouse, and so on. This disposition to innovate is also carried over into medical practices where we find these same individuals using more modern medical resources than their less-innovative neighbors. The use of these modern medical resources, however, comes into conflict with a number of previously entrenched beliefs. The traditional epistemology in Guatemala, as in many other parts of the world, has at its core numerous beliefs regarding the causes of illness and other misfortune which support and serve as a rationale for traditional medical practices. The use of modern medicine, which is based on quite different notions about the nature and causation of disease, is undermining these traditional beliefs. This is not dissimilar to the Yir Yiront case (page 23) where people started to doubt the validity of their origin myths and other beliefs when the steel axe could not be appropriately integrated into traditional patterns.

We should note in passing that, according to our model, traditional systems of belief are persistent to change even in the face of numerous technological innovations. They will begin to be questioned and dropped, though, following significant behavioral changes. In fact, while we cannot go into the technical aspects of the model here, it indicates that neither involvement in the cash economy, exposure to the outside world, nor a predisposition to innovate are *sufficient* to produce important changes in native epistemology. These shifts are dependent upon the behavioral change to modern medical practices.[7]

### RELIGIOUS CHANGE IN SAN PEDRO LA LAGUNA

In our discussion of the sequence of change in San Lucas we relied primarily on cross-sectional analysis. Our final example of change in highland Guatemala employs historical reconstruction along with a modified longitudinal approach to describe and explain the events which led to the dissolution of the religious fraternities, or *cofradías,* in San Pedro la Laguna. In terms of anthropological research, the town was first visited in 1936 by Sol Tax and then studied by a Guatemalan anthropologist, Juan de Dios Rosales, in 1938. Then, in 1941, Benjamin and Lois Paul began their work in San Pedro, returning many times in the succeeding years. These many return visits to San Pedro allow a longitudinal perspective on change as the Pauls were able to follow and record the many factors which finally led to the end of the *cofradías* system over the years. The account which follows is based primarily on the Pauls' work.[8]

San Pedro was described above as one of the most progressive towns on the lake. Indeed, it has undergone a number of significant changes over the last thirty-five years. In 1941 when the Pauls first entered the town the population consisted of about 1500 Mayan-speaking Indians wearing the distinctive community costume and practicing subsistence agriculture. Most of the population were nominal Catholics, there were no resident Ladinos, and no roads or paths connected them with the neighbor-

7. For more detailed information on the construction, testing, and implications of this processual model please refer to Clyde M. Woods and Theodore D. Graves, *The Process of Medical Change in a Highland Guatemalan Town,* Latin American Center, University of California at Los Angeles (1973).

8. See, particularly, Benjamin D. Paul, "San Pedro la Laguna," in *Los Pueblos del Lago Atitlán,* Sol Tax, ed. (Guatemala: Seminario de Integracion Social (1968) and Lois Paul and Benjamin D. Paul, "Changing Marriage Patterns in a Highland Guatemalan Community," *Southwest Journal of Anthropology* 19:131-48 (1963). Some of the information presented here is also based on personal communications with the Pauls.

ing towns. The civil-religious hierarchy was the mainstay of the social, religious, and political life of the community and only by moving from the lower to the higher positions in this institution could a man achieve the ultimate status accorded elders in the community.

As it existed, the hierarchy can be conceptualized as a ladder with two sets of rungs. The civil side of the ladder consists of a series of ranked political offices and the religous side a series of ranked ceremonial offices. Ideally, one progresses upwards rotating between the civil and religious sides of the ladder. Each new step up the ladder represents increased authority, respect, and prestige for the officeholder and his family and, at the same time, requires more investment in time and money. Terms of service are for one year with a four year period of rest in between each new office. At about the age of eighteen, young men would begin their cargo career as errand boys for the local government officials and firecracker donors for religious ceremonials. They would then work their way up the ladder through the various civil and ceremonial offices over the years until they reached the positions of mayor of the town and head of the most

important *cofradía*. At this point the highest status attainable within the community was awarded—that of *Principal*, or respected elder. This title remains the major life goal in traditional Mayan Indian communities.

The religious side of the hierarchy in San Pedro consisted of six ranked *confradías* which were each staffed by ten ranked officeholders. They were charged with maintaining the religious life of the community, sponsoring the annual round of fiestas, and venerating the saints. The civil side of the hierarchy was composed of eighteen offices ranging from errand boy or janitor through such responsibilities as membership on the town council to the final position of mayor. Both sides of the ladder were linked in that civil officeholders had religious functions and vice versa. In fact, the civil-religous split is a conceptual one imposed for descriptive purposes. The Indians themselves think of the hierarchy as a single system.

In sum, the civil-religious hierarchy served multiple and indispensable functions in San Pedro. It gave positive sanc-

9. This figure is based on personal communication with Benjamin D. Paul.

## FIGURE J

### THE COLLAPSE OF THE CIVIL-RELIGIOUS HIERARCHY IN SAN PEDRO[9]

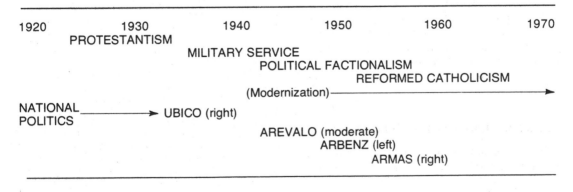

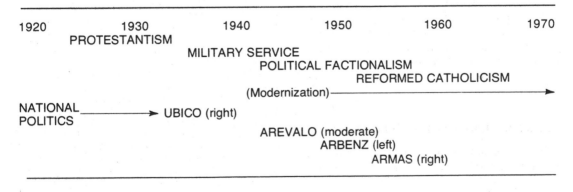

1920     1930     1940     1950     1960     1970
PROTESTANTISM
MILITARY SERVICE
POLITICAL FACTIONALISM
REFORMED CATHOLICISM
(Modernization)———————————————————>

NATIONAL
POLITICS————————> UBICO (right)
AREVALO (moderate)
ARBENZ (left)
ARMAS (right)

tion to authority, reinforced community integration, and generally served as a strong source of stability and conservatism. Over the years, however, a series of unpredictable events emanating both from within and without the community combined to knock the supports from the system and lead to its eventual collapse. The most important of these were (1) the growth of Protestantism, (2) military service, (3) political factionalism, (4) the reformed Catholic movement, and (5) the many influences of modernization. These events along with their approximate dates are plotted in Figure J.

According to Paul, Protestantism got its start around 1924 when a Pedrano who had begun to learn about the new religion experienced a "rags to riches" miracle. Already prospering, he became a true convert when his canoe capsized on the lake. When his pleas to the saints failed to help him, he tried Protestant prayers and was promptly rescued. Subsequently he started the first Protestant church. Divisiveness prevailed from the start as two of his converts started their own churches and others splintered from these. But the movement grew. By 1964, 33 percent of the population of San Pedro had joined one of the five denominations and by 1974 over 50 percent were divided into ten denominations. As mentioned earlier, conversion to Protestantism automatically prohibits *cofradía* service and some people took advantage of this by switching to one of the Protestant sects when it came time to serve. So the growth of Protestantism was a serious threat to the civil-religious hierarchy from the start.

Military service began in 1935 when San Pedro agreed to form the first volunteer military reserve company on the lake. They trained twice a week during the year and then marched to Guatemala City every summer for maneuvers. Later, military service became compulsory for many Ped-

ranos as Guatemala enacted conscription on a national level. The affects were manifold. Military service was translated by some into community service and they refused further offices in the hierarchy. Some stayed in the military for longer periods returning home literate, in modern dress, and with new occupations. Exposure to the outside world both on a limited and extended basis produced boredom with the traditional way of life in San Pedro.

National political changes also produced destructive effects locally. In 1944 Juan Jose Arévalo replaced Jorge Ubico as president of Guatemala. Under the rightest, conservative policies of Ubico the Indians had been left pretty much alone to manage their own affairs. Arévalo, however, instituted a series of liberal reforms which included the growth of political parties, a more tolerant attitude towards Protestantism, and the formal separation of church and state. At the local level this led to an official split in the civil-religious hierarchy and with the growth of political parties the younger, literate men moved into positions of political power. Hence, service in the system no longer guaranteed upward mobility as the younger men seized political power and left religious service for the older members of the community. In addition, a Protestant mayor got into power in San Pedro about this time. This gave impetus to the Protestant movement and created further factionalism in the community.

Arévalo was succeeded by Jacobo Arbenz Gusman in 1950 who continued his liberal programs with considerably increased vigor. A number of socialist reforms including the redistribution of land led to accusations that he was being heavily influenced by communism. These "leftist" tendencies upset the large landowners, foreign investors, and the United States government. Guatemala had gone "soft on communism" and so with the aid of the American government, a revolution was launched from the neighboring country of Honduras and Arbenz was overthrown and replaced by Castillo Armas in 1954. Armas was an arch-conservative, pro-Catholic president who abruptly ended the liberal programs initiated by his predecessors and launched an anti-Communist movement throughout the country. And, Protestants were commonly equated with Communists. Bloody purges took place at both local and national levels and given San Pedro's large Protestant population, factionalism and discontent increased. In 1957 Armas was assasinated by one of his guards. Military juntas ruled the country until regular elections were again established in the late sixties.

In the meantime, the reformed Catholic movement showed up on the lake in an attempt to reverse Protestant gains and purge Catholicism of its pagan elements. In San Pedro many turned to this new group and they too became ineligible for service in the traditional religious offices because many of their practices were equated with paganism. This led to factionalism among the Catholics and further community dissension. The final blow, perhaps, was the coming of a resident Catholic priest. He took the saints out of the *cofradías* and put them in the church, placed the maintenance of the church and religious activities under the auspices of the reformed Catholic membership, and moved against many of the *cofradía* activities such as dancing and drinking during fiestas. The Protestants had gained an effective ally.

A number of related changes contributed further to the breakdown of the *cofradía* system. Coffee became a major cash crop around 1926 and Pedranos acquired about one-half of the land in neighboring San Juan. A spurt of business activity followed as new businesses were opened and San Pedro spread its entrepreneurial activities outside the local area. Considering all the other influences working against service in the *cofradías*, Pedranos became more and more skeptical of spending their new wealth on community service. Then in 1954 regular boat cargo and passenger service was established with Panajachel and in 1958 the road came in. Communication with the outside world increased commensurately and modernization followed suit. The *cofradías* continued to function on a limited basis through the 1960s and in 1971 this writer was able to obtain a list of the names of all the *cofradía* heads even though there was no further membership and obstensibly no function. By 1973 tradition had bowed to the winds of change and the *cofradías* in San Pedro la Laguna were no longer existent.

San Pedro, in 1974, is the only town on the lake without these religious fraternities. In other towns changes have occured in these institutions but they have survived in one form or another. In some towns the religious fraternities have merged with the reformed Catholics to carry on the social and religious life of the community (San Juan and San Marcos) while in others the fraternities continue to function as in the past but have no significant ties with the civil hierarchy (San Lucas and Santiago). But in some the fraternities remain virtually intact and continue to maintain the social, religious, and political life in the community (San Antonio and Santa Cruz).

## SUMMARY

This final chapter described development, modernization, and change in general, as they are taking place in the midwestern highlands of Guatemala. The intent was to use this material to further examine the dimensions of community development and modernization presented in the previous chapter, and by way of general summary, the overall dynamics of sociocultural change. Descriptive materials on this region were provided earlier. Here we started by presenting the design of an ongoing study of change focused on the Mayan Indian towns located around Lake Atitlán. Ten of these towns were placed on a developmental continuum and rank-ordered on development, exposure, population size, and relative traditionality. We discussed some anomalies in the data and concluded that, in light of these, the four orderings were fairly well related. Exposure, however, was clearly the best indicator of development. Six of these towns were then rank-ordered on various measures of individual modernization so that development and modernization could be compared. Similar anomalies in the data were discussed and we concluded that the two processes were related but that the relationship was far from perfect. Considering only modernization, we found that the process was a fairly unified one but that there were obvious lags between different areas of change. We then turned to an investigation of change in two of the towns. In San Lucas we examined medical and related changes, and in San Pedro we focused on the many events which led to drastic changes in the social, political, and religious life of the community. These case studies not only showed the process of medical and religious change in the two towns, but were meant to illustrate many of the principles of change outlined throughout the book.

### For Further Reading

Nash, M., ed. *Handbook of Middle American Indians*, vol. 6. Austin: University of Texas Press, 1967. Readings on the social anthropology of middle American Indians which vary in quality but provide useful information on culture and society in this area of the world. See particularly the chapters on "Indian Economies" and "Political and Religious Organizations."

Nash, M. *Machine Age Maya*. Chicago: University of Chicago Press, 1958. In addition to providing a lot of useful descriptive materials on a Mayan Indian community, Nash shows how the introduction of a textile factory in the town of Cantel did not disrupt traditional cultural patterns.

Reina, R. *Chinautla: A Guatemalan Indian Community*. New Orleans: Tulane University, Middle American Research Institute, Publication 24, 1960. Basically an ethnography of the community, Reina agrees with Nash (above) that traditional patterns are little effected by the introduction of Western technological items.

Tax, S. *Penny Capitalism: A Guatemalan Indian Economy*. Washington, D.C.: Smithsonian Institute, Institute of Social Anthropology, Publication 16, 1953. This is a classic study of the Indian economy in the town of Panajachel on Lake Atitlán and Tax's findings can be generalized to other towns in the area as well.

Tax, S., ed. *Los Pueblos del Lago Atitlán*. Guatemala: Seminario de Integracion Social, 1968. This book, written by American and Guatemalan anthropologists, considers changes in the towns of Lake Atitlán in the midwestern highlands of Guatemala over a twenty-five-year period. Unfortunately, it is only available in Spanish.

Vogt, E. Z., ed. *Handbook of Middle American Indians*, vol. 7, part 1. Austin: University of Texas Press, 1969. These collected essays deal with the ethnology of Middle American Indians. See, particularly, the first five chapters dealing with the Mayans of the western highlands of Guatemala.

Woods, C. M. and T. D. Graves *The Process of Medical Change in a Highland Guatemalan*

*Town.* Latin American Center, University of California at Los Angeles 1973. This short monograph presents basic ethnographic material, compares Indian and Ladino life-styles, considers the direction of change in the community, and proposes a processual, or sequential, model of the change process.

## Bibliography

Paul, B. D. 1968. "San Pedro la Laguna." In *Los Pueblos del Lago Atitlán,* ed. Sol Tax, Guatemala: Seminario de Integracion Social.

Paul, L. and Paul, B. D. 1963. "Changing Marriage Patterns in a Highland Guatemalan Community." *Southwestern Journal of Anthropology* 19: 131-148.

Tax, S. 1946. *The Towns of Lake Atitlán.* Chicago: University of Chicago Library. Microfilm Collection of Manuscripts on Middle American Cultural Anthropology, 13.

Woods, C. M. and Graves, T. D. 1973. *The Process of Medical Change in a Highland Guatemalan Town.* Los Angeles: Latin American Center, University of California at Los Angeles.

# Glossary

**Accidental Juxtaposition**—The process whereby two or more previously unrelated ideas or objects are accidentally brought together so that something new is created.

**Acculturation**—Change which occurs when two or more previously autonomous cultural traditions come into continuous contact with sufficient intensity to promote extensive changes in one or more.

**Age-Area Hypothesis**—The notion that traits and complexes found furthest from their proposed place of origin diffused earlier and are therefore older.

**American Historical School**—A school of diffusion which used the culture area concept to make limited historical reconstructions.

**Assimilation**—The process whereby two or more previously separate cultural traditions are combined to produce something new.

**Civil-Religious Hierarchy**—An institution composed of a series of ranked and interrelated civil and ceremonial offices which maintain the political, social, and religious life of Guatemalan Indian communities.

**Classical Evolution**—Early school of anthropology which proposed that cultures everywhere progressed through the same stages in unilineal fashion because of the fact that man's mental processes were universally the same.

**Cofradía**—The religious side of the civil-religious hierarchy, also referred to as religious fraternities, composed of a series of ranked ceremonial offices.

**Community Development**—Process whereby a contemporary society improves its control of the environment by means of an increasingly competent technology applied by increasingly complex organizations.

**Concept**—Abstractions from concrete observations which serve as the basic building blocks, or elements, of theory.

**Cross-Sectional Analysis**—A method whereby change can be inferred by focusing on the range of variability within and/or between societies.

**Cultural Relativity**—The notion that practices should only be evaluated in terms of the cultural setting in which they take place.

**Culture**—An integrated system of learned behavior patterns which are characteristic of the members of a society and are not the result of biological inheritance; prescriptions for behavior in the mind of man, some of which are shared and some of which are not.

75

**Culture Area**—A common cultural tradition sharing a common ecological niche.

**Culture Change**—Any modification in the way of life of a people whether consequent to internal developments or to contact between peoples with unlike ways of life: modifications in individual prescriptions for behavior.

**Culture Circle School**—A school of diffusion which proposed that culture developed in different parts of the world and then spread from these hearths to other areas, coming into contact as they spread thereby accelerating the process of borrowing.

**Culture Climax**—The most favorable ecological niche within a given culture area where the culture is most elaborated and where the dominant patterns are absorbed, recreated, and radiated outward. Also referred to as the culture focus.

**Culture Complex**—A series of functionally related culture traits.

**Culture trait**—A single, and supposedly irreducible, element of culture.

**Culturology**—The notion that culture is superorganic in that it evolves sui generis, according to its own laws, and apart from the influence of its bearers.

**Diffusion**—The process whereby traits or complexes spread from one society or group to another.

**Discovery**—The act of becoming aware of something which has been in existence but previously unperceived.

**Directed Change**—The active and purposeful intervention of individuals or groups into the practices of other peoples. Also referred to as applied anthropology within the context of the discipline.

**Ecological Adaptation**—The relationship between cultural practices and the geographical environment in which they occur including the influence each bears on the other. Also referred to as cultural-ecological adaptation.

**Empathy**—The ability to imagine one's self in the roles of others.

**Environmental Modification**—A change in the sociocultural (man, culture, and society) or the physical (natural or man-made) environment.

**Fatalism**—The degree to which an individual feels that he has control over his own destiny.

**General Evolution**—An interest in broad scale trends in cultural evolution.

**Homogeneity Postulate**—The notion that people in a given society or group are more or less exact replicas of one another and their culture.

**Historical Reconstruction**—Reconstruction of the past based on the use of written documents, the archaeological record, and informant recall.

**Ideal Concept**—Conceptualizations based on observations of reality but generalized or standardized so as to make comparisons possible.

**Independent Invention**—Invention of the same thing in different places with no evidence of contact or influence between them.

**Innovation**—Any thought, behavior, or thing that is new because it is qualitatively different from existing forms.

**Innovators**—Those members of a given society or group who adopt innovations first.

**Intercultural Variation**—Differences between groups or societies.

**Intracultural Variation**—Differences within groups or societies.

**Invention**—A new synthesis of preexistent materials, conditions, or practices.

**Ladino**—The non-Indian segment of Guatemalan society who claim varying degrees of Spanish ancestry. Also used to refer to any non-Indian regardless of place of origin, such as North Americans, Italians, etc.

**Ladinoization**—The acculturation process in Guatemala whereby Indians shed their traditional way of life and pass into the Ladino class.

**Longitudinal**—With regard to the study of change, an approach whereby similar information is gathered on members of the same group over an extended period of time.

**Long-Term Variation**—The process whereby gradual accumulations and slight modifications over extended periods of time result in something qualitatively new. Also referred to, in general, as evolution.

**Modernization**—The process whereby individuals change from a traditional to a more complex, technologically advanced, and rapidly changing way of life.

**Multilinear Evolution**—A limited form of the application of evolution in which cross-cultural regularities in the change process are sought and which proposes that similar causes lead to like effects.

**Multivariate**—The use of multiple variables and the relationships between them to explain or investigate a particular research problem.

**Neoevolution**—A contemporary school of evolution which searches for broad scale trends in the succession of cultural forms but does not adhere to the rigid laws proposed by the classical evolutionists.

**Pan-Egyptian School**—A school of diffusion which proposed that culture developed in Egypt and spread from there to the rest of the world.

**Participant Intervention**—A term coined by the Cornell-Vicos project to describe their planned and active intervention into the practices of the people in Vicos, Peru in the context of a directed change program.

**Psychic Unity of Mankind**—The notion that man's mental processes are universally the same.

**Reactive Movements**—Native reactions to change generalized in anthropology as *revitalization movements* and defined as deliberate, organized, conscious efforts by members of a society to construct a more meaningful culture.

**Reinterpretation**—The alteration of newly introduced traits and complexes in form, function, and meaning by members of the receiving group.

**Shaman**—The anthropological gloss for traditional curing practitioners who, in the Guatemalan case, may practice healing, witchcraft, or both.

**Social Change**—Modifications in the structure and/or function of the social system.

**Social System**—The patterns of social interaction which occur within a given society.

**Sociocultural Change**—A term which glosses both cultural and social change change into a single process.

**Specific Evolution**—An interest in limited manifestations of general societal evolution.

**Stimulus Diffusion**—The process whereby the idea for a new practice is borrowed but the actual content is not.

**Study-Restudy**—An approach to the study of change whereby the same society is studied at two or more points in time.

**Syncretism**—The process whereby traits from previously separated cultural traditions are combined to produce something new.

**Temascal**—The Spanish term for an Indian sweat bath.

# Index